Social Media Marketing

Learn How to Become a Skilled Influencer on Facebook, Instagram, YouTube, and Twitter

Top Digital Networking and Personal Branding Strategies

Jason Miller

Text Copyright © 2020 Jason Miller

All rights reserved.

No part of this guide may be reproduced in any form without permission in writing from the publisher except in the case of brief quotations embodied in critical articles or reviews.

Legal & Disclaimer:

The information contained in this book and its contents is not designed to replace or take the place of any form of medical or professional advice; and is not meant to replace the need for independent medical, financial, legal or other professional advice or services, as may be required. The content and information in this book has been provided for educational and entertainment purposes only.

The content and information contained in this book has been compiled from sources deemed reliable, and it is accurate to the best of the Author's knowledge, information and belief. However, the Author cannot guarantee its accuracy and validity and cannot be held liable for any errors and/or omissions. Further, changes are periodically made to this book as and when needed. Where appropriate and/or necessary, you must consult a professional (including but not limited to your doctor, attorney, financial advisor or such other professional advisor) before using any of the suggested remedies, techniques, or information in this book.

Upon using the contents and information contained in this book, you agree to hold harmless the Author from and against any damages, costs, and expenses, including any legal fees potentially resulting from the application of any of the information provided by this book. This disclaimer applies to any loss, damages or injury caused by the use and application, whether directly or indirectly, of any advice or information presented, whether for breach of contract, tort, negligence, personal injury, criminal intent, or under any other cause of action.

Table of Contents

Introduction — 6

Chapter 1: The Concept Of Social Media Marketing And Its Evolution — 8

What is Social Media Marketing? 8

Social Media History — 10

Social Media Marketing Importance 11

Chapter 2: Social Media Trends for 2021 — 14

1. Goodbye to Likes on Instagram 15
2. Ephemeral content 15
3. Niche social networks 16
4. Social Shopping 16
5. Video content 16
6. Segmentation with artificial intelligence 17
7. Augmented Reality 17
8. Customer service 18
9. Increased security and privacy controls 18
10. Local actions 18
11. Social Listening 19
12. User-generated content 20
13. Focus on engagement 21
14. Groups and Communities 21
Why use social media and SEO for your brand 21
Advertising with Influencers and ten benefits 24

Chapter 3: Building your core brand strategy — 26

Brands live in the minds of buyers 26
Step #1: Define your strategy 28
Step #2: Logo 33

Step #3: Naming... 37
Step #4: Your brand 41
Step #5: Brand positioning 43
Step #6: Brand loyalty 48

Chapter 4: Content Marketing 53

Content Inbound Marketing 54

Chapter 5: Facebook Marketing 62

Facebook Statistics 63
Customer interaction 64
SEO 66
Free Promotion 68
Responding To Problems 71
Beating Your Competition 73
Facebook Ads 78

Chapter 6: LinkedIn Marketing 87

How To Use Linkedin For Your Business Or Success 87
Advertising Opportunities 92

Chapter 7: Instagram Marketing 100

How To Market On Instagram 100
A Brief Comparison To Snapchat 107
How Instagram Is Like Twitter With Picture 109

Chapter 8: YouTube Marketing 111

How To Market On YouTube? 111
Tools For YouTube 115

Chapter 9: Marketing on Pinterest 119

Ecommerce Stores And Retailers Data......................... 119

Six strategies to use Pinterest in your business effectively 120
Best practices on Pinterest 123
How to direct traffic from Pinterest to your website or blog 124

Chapter 10: Other Marketing Tools To Get Success 125

Marketing Automation Tool 125
Email Marketing Tool 125
Landing page creation tool 127
Content Marketing Platform 127
Local SEO and Review Marketing 127
Analytics tool 128
CMS (Content Management System) 128
Social Media Monitoring Tool 128

Chapter 11: New Ways To Social And Go Marketing 129

What To Do 129
What Not To Do 130

Conclusion   132

Introduction

Social Media Marketing is a marketing branch that starts with commercial strategies designed to take advantage of its possible tools when developing its social network activity. An extension that also has become especially important in recent years.

The large number of users who move on platforms such as Twitter, Facebook, or even Instagram has led to this type of marketing becoming one of the main strengths in any strategy carried out today. The ease of achieving a great reach, and the potential to achieve a greater connection with the audience has been its primary triggers.

Social networks have become one of the main focuses of study for marketers[1]. Developing a good strategy in these digital environments is not something that depends only on the message. It also depends on how launched, how it is established and before which eyes it is found. It requires an in-depth prior study and an excellent knowledge of both the audience and the type of user that move through the platform in question.

The complexity of Marketing in social media is more significant than it seems at first glance. For that reason, it is not surprising that there are figures such as specialists in Social Media focused on getting the most out of social media. Now, the question is the following:

What is Social Media Marketing for?

Social media Marketing serves, in the first place, to get closer to the public. Given the easy interaction enhanced in this environment, the

---

[1] Constantinides, Efthymios, Lorenzo, Carlota, Alarcon-del-Amo, María-del-Carmen (2013/01/01). Social Networking Sites as Business Tool: A Study of User Behavior. Business Process Management; Studies in Computational Intelligence (book).444 221-240.DOI: 10.1007/978-3-642-28409-0_9

connection between brand and consumer can be made directly, with hardly any complications.

Thus, campaigns can be launched with a high success rate but also generate interest in the brand. The number of leads is increased relatively quickly, and, above all, the brand image is enhanced. The latter is the most exciting point and can most be promoted with social media strategies.

There are many examples of social media marketing since many brands and users move into the digital sector's environments. Initiatives take place daily with proposals and ideas of all kinds, some more and others less effective.

This book will see specific cases; you will find examples of successful campaigns on social networks.

This book is for you if you are looking for more information on social media marketing. Through related content, I will offer you a guide to help you take action if you want to use social media marketing.

I suggest you to continue reading my book until the end. Please take a look at the links to expand and learn more about it and other essential elements in this field. I hope you can take advantage of it.

Enjoy it!

Chapter 1

The Concept Of Social Media Marketing And Its Evolution

Social Networks or Social Media presents a wide range of opportunities for companies to reach any corner of the world. How? To be successful in social networks, you have to set an Online Marketing strategy according to its business objectives (create a brand, get contacts, increase sales or retain customers, for example), and use the audience's social networks. However, the essential keys are the main objective and planning of the marketing campaign, since some networks are more prepared than others in a specific aspect, such as, for example, e-commerce sales are more useful on Facebook than On Twitter. Likewise, the choice of social networks (Facebook, Twitter, Instagram, LinkedIn, or YouTube) will depend on the company, its objectives, and its main product. An excellent social media marketing strategy is very clear about why and what to use each social media for; It is not about trying to be everywhere, but about approaching your potential customers with the social networks that are most useful for your company and being active in them, offering quality and exciting content.

What is Social Media Marketing?

Before popularizing social networks on the internet, marketing strategies were carried out mainly in traditional media. In this way, radio or television, paper newspapers, flyers, among other channels, were used to communicate with the public.

These media had a disadvantage: the power of communication was only in the hands of a few. Thus, the owners of television networks, for example, were the only ones who could produce content for that vehicle. In such a way that if the companies wanted to issue a statement, display an advertising message... they had to pay for it to be published.

With the popularization of social networks on the internet, companies could have their communication channels. Today, anyone can create an account on YouTube and produce videos, for example.

But, the concept of social media marketing is vast. It refers to the production of content for all the media that have emerged. It must also be aware of the relationship with the public.

Today, anyone can enter an organization's Facebook page and leave a negative message. In this case, it is necessary to use public relations techniques to defuse the situation and prevent it from becoming a disruption or an image crisis for the company.

Also, budget planning and control must always be taken into account in social media marketing tasks. Just as in the past, it was necessary to pay to appear on television, now there are also means to make sponsored posts and advertisements on most social networks. In this way, the publications reach a larger number of people.

What are the advantages of social media marketing?

The main advantage of investing in advertising on social networks is that they are not massive. If you have a company that sells articles for athletes, for example, and you buy an ad in primetime on the largest radio station in Chile, it will have tremendous visibility. Hundreds of thousands of people will see your ad! But how many are interested in what you sell?

In social networks, you can make the same ad and segment it towards a much more restricted audience profile of people interested in acquiring the products for athletes you are selling.

It justifies why classifications can be created according to sex, age, location, preferences registered in the social networks themselves. In this way, your money will be well spent, and the results will be more useful for your business.

Social networks give us specific information about potential buyers to know what we should offer them and thus increase sales.

Social Media has an exact online results measurement system, so SME's maSMEs'ting strategy improved based on the data provided by social networks.

Social Media History

According to various authors, the first social network that was in operation was classmates.com. The idea came from Randy Conrads in 1995, and the website sought to connect former classmates from college, institute, or university. His popularity was imminent, and Conrads was recognized with awards such as eBusiness Reports 2001 Entrepreneur of the Year.

This network was preceded by sixdegrees.com (1997) and Open Diary (1998). The first was a social network based on the six degrees of separation, and the second will be the first blogging community on the internet.

Another significant milestone was Blogger's (1999) emergence, a blogging service created by the Pyra Labs company and the term blog. This service was acquired in 2003 by Google.

In 2002 DeviantArt appeared from three engineers: Scott Jarkoff, Angelo Sotira, and Matthew Stephens. This website was born to create an international community of artists on the web. This space gained popularity among different artists, having in 2007 some 4.5 million users and 50 million creations. In February 2017, it was acquired by wix.com for $ 36 million.

The next space that was looking to create virtual communities was Friendster. In 2002, two computer programmers from California launched a new dating website under the name match.com. It differed from the rest of this style's portals in that the contact between two people was made for similar hobbies or to share acquaintances.

Its popularity grew dramatically, achieving millions of registrations in months, receiving a purchase offer from Google just a year after its creation. However, several factors caused the massive exit of users. Among the main factors were: privacy problems, an architecture that is difficult to scale, and the community's rebellion to its rules.

In 2003, the Social Network boom began, and websites such as tribe.net, MySpace, Ecademy, Soflow, Xing, hi5, Netlog, and LinkedIn appeared. There were already more than 200 social media platforms at this time, but each one was weaving its niche, positioning itself and differentiate itself from each other.

Among those that stand out in this wave of social networks is undoubtedly My Space, a site for lovers of music and artistic trends. It was one of the most famous in its time; between 2005 and 2008, it was the most visited social network globally.

As of 2004, other famous ones like Flickr, Tagged, Orkut, and the crown's queen are added: Facebook. In 2005 Reddit appeared, and Yahoo launched its social network that included a blog and Flickr photo album, which closed in 2009 without much success.

Twitter, Badoo, and Tuenti were born in 2006 and Tumblr in 2007. Until 2010, Instagram appears as one of the most popular currently and acquired in 2012 by Facebook. Lastly, Pinterest stood out, and Google's incorporation into the market with Google+ in 2011.

Social Media Marketing Importance

Companies always tend to have a bigger goal in mind, and that is to increase sales. That's why companies do everything they do: improve product quality, offer reasonable prices, invest in marketing, and more.

For this reason, including the use of social networks in a marketing plan is so important: Because it directly helps to increase the sales of a company, almost instantly.

Proper use of social media not only allows you to gain greater exposure to people who may not have even known your company before, but it also allows them to interact with you in a much more direct way.

Marketing is an activity that aims to identify the needs and desires of the market to adapt and offer the desired satisfactions. If the market evolves, marketing must respond to it. Thus, digital marketing has changed its "formula" with the entry of social networks' dynamics.

The Social Media Plans are current processes and in constant reinvention. Its objective is to promote a brand through social networks to reach a target audience with a personalized and dynamic message. Its primary tool is content in different formats.

Networks are platforms for socializing and are not advertising platforms, where traditional marketing actions were commonly carried out. Thus, the focus changes, and selling is no longer the main priority on these platforms. With them, we seek to obtain useful information to attract new customers.

Social media brought with it the 4Cs of marketing

Content: the key to any Social Media strategy, the content must be authentic, of value, and capture the attention of potential customers.

Context: Each social network has a way of being. In other words, the message to be transmitted to the user must be placed in the context of our potential client's life cycle.

Community: from the creation of quality content, identifying influencers and interacting with people, a commitment to the brand and the gestation of the community is fostered. It is where an engagement takes its principal value.

Connections: the investigation must be active in social networks. It is essential to listen and be aware of the latest statistics. Social networks are not static. They are dynamic structures that respond to people's experiences.

Chapter 2

Social Media Trends for 2021

The year 2019 is over, 2020 is almost over, and with it are some trends in social networks that were fashionable these years, and others are here to stay.

Are you already preparing your company's digital strategy for next year? And what about social media? Do you want to know what will be on social networks this 2020?

Well, do not miss this section where I will explain them to you.

1. Goodbye to Likes on Instagram

Instagram, the fashion social network during 2018 and 2019, plans to implement one of the most significant changes in social networks: eliminating "likes."

The disappearance of that button is, at best, controversial:

Many users use the social network to validate its popularity and social value. And in many cases, the obsession with the like leads some users to do foolish things. In case of not having enough likes, some users suffer a decrease in self-esteem and even mental health problems.

It is the main reason why Instagram considers it necessary to remove likes from its social network.

However, many claims that removing likes is an Instagram strategy to earn money since by not knowing the preferences that publications receive, they will not measure the impact of their campaigns with influencers. At least not as easy as so far.

In this way, advertising on Instagram will be the safest ROI for brands.

Whatever the reason, the truth is that this change will be a trend and will affect the use that brands make of their social media marketing strategy.

2. Ephemeral content

The creation and consumption of ephemeral content grow year after year: from the popularization of Snapchat among the youngest to the success of Instagram Stories or Facebook Stories.

The trend of creating short, engaging, entertaining, and short-lived content is here to stay.

According to a Hootsuite study, 64% of marketers have already incorporated Instagram Stories into their Social Media strategy this year.

3. Niche social networks

Everyone, or almost, has an account on one of the generic social networks. But the niche social networks that are also very popular and have great engagement among their followers: from Linkedin, the work social network, or Pinterest, the inspirational social network, through the new social networks that triumph among Generation Z for example, Twitch, the gaming social network or Tik Tok, the music video social network.

Therefore, it will not be strange that these 2020 brands include niche social networks in their social media marketing strategy.

4. Social Shopping

Users are making more and more purchases online. And although until recently, social networks were not a place to buy directly, today there are already many platforms such as Instagram, Pinterest, Facebook, ... that offer the possibility of selling now.

Also, social networks focused on the display and sale of products have proliferated. So the trend of Social Shopping has also come to stay.

The main winners of this trend are Fashion items, travel, movies, music, and electronics.

So if your company sells any of these products, we recommend that you include Social Shopping this year in your digital strategy.

5. Video content

Video content continues to grow year after year. YouTube is still one of the most important social networks. And in the success of Tik Tok, we can see the rise of video as a content format among the new generations.

According to a Cisco study, by 2020, 82% of the content will be video.

Of course, not any type of video will work. Those videos should be designed primarily for social networks, which implies videos without audio, and vertically for stories and square or horizontal videos for posts. Click here. You will find 11 best on Biteable.

6. Segmentation with artificial intelligence

Artificial intelligence is penetrating more and more in our day-to-day. And social networks are not out of this trend.

There is more and more content. And it is becoming more and more complicated for social media algorithms to discern between good and bad content, false content.

For this reason, social platforms are working on smarter algorithms that are capable of better evaluating the quality of the content that is shared.

In 2021 we will start to see it as part of Fake News, and sensitive content will be filtered directly by the new algorithms.

It will also be increasingly common to see how automatic chatbots are introduced into networks: Facebook Messenger to WhatsApp Business.

7. Augmented Reality

Augmented reality is also a trend that is here to stay.

Snapchat became fashionable; this trend has been growing and penetrating different social networks: Instagram, Facebook ...

That is why it is not surprising that augmented reality filters proliferate. But also the posts and stories of augmented reality.

It will open a new field of action for brands that will publicize and even give their products a try thanks to augmented reality on social networks.

8. Customer service

Many brands only consider social networks as a sales tool. However, this year we will see how using social networks as post-sale tools grow, seeking to improve the user experience and build loyalty.

The use of chatbots and management platforms for companies will make it possible for brands to use social networks as a direct and instant communication tool to offer personalized pre- and post-sale attention.

9. Increased security and privacy controls

News of the sale of Facebook data to private companies and the inappropriate use of that data by third parties has made both Facebook and the rest of social networks in the spotlight.

As a result, both Facebook and other social platforms have committed to user data security by tightening their security controls and adding new privacy policies.

Furthermore, if we add to this the proliferation of Fake News and the struggle of social networks to filter them before they go viral, they will continue to increase the security and control of social networks in 2020.

10. Local actions

The geolocation of many social networks makes it possible to carry out local Social Media strategies.

This option is very interesting for brands with physical businesses that need to carry out actions in particular places. Keep in mind that thanks to geolocated advertising on social networks, brands will carry out activities on social networks only with those in a radius or a specific place.

11. Social Listening

Brands are increasingly aware of how important it is to know your users. Social networks offer brands the possibility of listening to the user, interacting with him, identifying comments, learning opinions, discovering data, trends, profiles, and evaluating a company, ...

@torreseric27 I think we're going to have to direct to @adidas for that one 😊

All this information is vital for brands since it allows us to readjust the company's marketing and communication strategy and create campaigns and actions that genuinely work.

For this reason, Social Listening will be a growing trend over the years. And with it, the fast and personalized campaigns created to respond to specific comments from one or some users at a particular time who are giving something to talk about on social networks.

12. User-generated content

With social networks, the Prosumer was born. That is the consumer who is also a content producer.

Source: medialuv.com

In the future, you will see how more and more brands are encouraged to use the content created by their customers and users on their social networks.

We will also see how the brands themselves encourage users to create content as part of its advertising campaign.

In this way, brands will be able to go viral in a non-intrusive way and, at the same time, improve their reputation since the content created by users is more credible for other users than that generated by the brands. Click on 5 Effective Ways User-Generated Content Can Boost Traffic to learn more.

13. Focus on engagement

With the like button's disappearance from some social networks, users' focus will increase by getting as many comments as possible, clicks that redirect to a specific website, insertions of a particular hashtag, or mentions of a brand.

In turn, it will make brands focus on seeking the maximum possible engagement to measure the success of their campaigns and actions.

Likewise, we will see how the most demanded influencers will achieve the most significant engagement with their users.

14. Groups and Communities

During 2019 and 2020, we have seen how Facebook groups would have happened. And over the next years, we will see how communities within social networks become commonplace, as they allow users to share experiences, discuss certain topics, exchange opinions, seek solutions to specific problems.

For this reason, many brands will choose to create their community groups to do Social Listening and, at the same time, be able to promote their products or services when they consider it appropriate.

As you have seen, 2021 will be a very social year.

Are you going to implement any of these trends in your company's Social Media strategy? Here are some tips to help you stand out on social media.

Why use social media and SEO for your brand

It is vital to understand the operation of social networks and your audience's response in each of them, analyzing, evaluating, and executing the content. That is why we share some reasons why marketing is vital on your social networks. First, let's talk about why you must use social media. We can mention four keys reasons.

Brand building

As a brand, we must attract and satisfy our audience predictably and consistently to generate empathy with our consumers. One of the best ways to do this is by offering content that enriches them both intellectually and emotionally to build a strong and positive brand in our audience's minds.

Web traffic

We are talking about the number of visitors who access our website and add value to our digital portal. Using a good social media strategy is an excellent way to attract visitors to our site from well-known platforms such as Facebook, Twitter, Linkedin, and many more.

Positioning (SEO)

More traffic to our site means a better reputation when search engines decide to do the positioning job. Likewise, the activity of our social profiles adds value to our brand in the digital world. A site with higher external references has a better page rank for search engines.

Return on investment (ROI)

Social networks are powerful tools, and marketing on them represents a much lower cost than other digital and traditional media. In addition to being cheaper, the segmentation it offers is specific and accurate, which allows us to reach our target market more quickly, making our brand more relevant and the purchase intention more significant.

Simply put, social media marketing is key to growing your brand today. If your brand does not yet have web positioning strategies, now is the time to start.

SEO for your brand

Performing your business's SEO web positioning is currently going to be a key piece in your business's success. Next, we show you why it is essential to make the right organic search engine positioning strategies for your website or business.

1. More visibility of our website

The first thing we want to achieve, and achieved with a good web positioning technique, is to increase our website's visibility. A fundamental strategy so that our public can contact us more easily. Also, we managed to empower and grow the audience of our website.

This audience grows because when users search for terms related to our website or business, Google positions our website among the top positions on the results page.

The first thing we have to do to achieve more visibility is to choose the terms that we will position as keywords in search engines. When we have this list of keywords to place, we will focus our SEO strategy on it, and thus we will achieve that when someone searches for those words in Google, our page will appear among the first results.

For example, if we are a company that sells furniture, we must choose the keywords most related to those that the user who is looking for furniture would prefer in their search.

2. Increase the number of visits

If we manage to increase visibility, the next step we will achieve will be to increase the number of visits to our website. Thus, enhancing the visibility of our business on the internet.

When our website is visible, it appears among the first results of Google. It will be possible that the user enters your page; thus, increasing the number of visits potentially.

3. We achieve goals

We have already managed to increase our time's visibility and, therefore, we have increased the number of visits to our page. With this, we will have also managed to increase conversions, that is, to improve the achievement of objectives. We achieve conversions when, for example, the user fills in a form, completes a purchase, shares a publication, or interacts, in any way, with our website. Any action carried out by the user can be a conversion for our website if it is configured like this previously.

Therefore, we will achieve more conversions for our website the more visibility and visits our website has. A good strategy would undoubtedly be to orient the web design towards conversions, taking the results where the brand wants.

Advertising with Influencers and ten benefits

Advertising with Influencers is also a trend. Thanks to social networks, the use of influencers and micro-influencers has proliferated in online marketing strategies.

And this trend will continue to be very present in 2020, where even more brands will join in with influencers to promote their brands and products.

The trend of brands for this year will go through working with more micro-influencers instead of prominent influencers.

Ten benefits of working with our brand with specific influencers

1. Their recommendations have more credibility than conventional advertising in physical and digital media

2. They help us to publicize our brand or our products
3. They help us increase the credibility of our brand and our products
4. Encourage positive word of mouth about our brand and products
5. They allow us to reach our potential audience in a non-intrusive way and with maximum credibility
6. They add value to our brand, humanize it and make it close to our clients and future clients
7. Help differentiate our brand from the competition
8. It allows us to promote direct sales of certain products quickly and effectively
9. It helps us to improve the organic positioning of our website in search engines (SEO)
10. It will improve the profitability of our digital campaigns since influencers are very profitable for brands (investment-benefit ratio)

Of course, the key to the success of campaigns with influencers and micro-influencers will be choosing the most appropriate influencer for your brand. Click here to find some tips on how to select the best influencers for your brand.

Chapter 3

Building your core brand strategy

A brand is a name, term, design, symbol, or any other characteristic that identifies a seller's goods and services and formally differentiates them from their competition. (American Marketing Association). The brand is a symbol of trust. When consumers trust and believe in a brand, they hardly look for new alternatives.

Brands live in the minds of buyers

Brands have a special meaning. Based on past experiences with the product and its years of the marketing program, consumers know which brands meet their needs and which do not. The set of affairs in the use of products, with advertising, with references, conversations, accompanied by dreams and aspirations, are the ingredients in constructing brands and their fixation in mind.

There are many types of associations that refer us to the brand: there are many different ways to create them. The entire marketing program can help consumers understand the brand and influence how they evaluate, feel, and identify with it.

By building branding and developing customer loyalty, perceived differences are created between different products, and thus marketers create value that can translate into financial returns for the business.

A Brand is a complex symbol. It is the intangible sum of a product's attributes, name, image, packaging, and price. Its history, reputation, and the way it is promoted. A brand is also defined by consumers' perception, the people who use it, and their own experiences.

Branding, what for?

Do you know what is the second most well-known word in the world after, OK? Coca Cola. Surprised? Probably not. The secret? This company has understood very well what it is about developing a Branding strategy and, above all, how to do it.

These are some of the key points that make up its Branding strategy and that make 70% of the company's value correspond to its brand:

Tell a story: From its emergence as a medicine to the myth about the ingredients that make up its formula, Coca Cola linked to great stories.

Associate the brand with emotions and positive values: Eternally linked to happiness and family unity.

Constantly renewing itself, adapting to the new conditions of the context: The company was one of the first to disembark in the beautiful but uncertain world 2.0. It quickly understood the principles that govern it, and it knew how to take advantage of them. It uses social networks, app development, and new technologies to connect with its audience through creative and fun actions.

The cleverness to be present in the places where its public is: Coca-Cola regularly organizes music, sporting events, and competitions. Now it even has its radio station to communicate with its target.

The question you must be asking yourself now is… how I can do the same with my company?

The answer is simple: defining your Branding strategy step by step. Let's start!

The goal of Marketing is to get people to know you, love you, and trust you. One of the best ways to make yourself known and get loved is by introducing yourself. The design of a brand involves defining how you want to show yourself to others.

Why think about branding? The right answer is: the brand's perception directly affects the value assigned to it and customers' behavior.

People are willing to pay more for products from well-positioned brands, as they believe they will be more beneficial than others. Not only that, but they are also more likely to buy that product again.

It is because a very particular type of bond is generated between the brand and its audiences. It means more customers, more income. Correctly defining a branding strategy will allow you to:

- Reach the customer with a clear message, without the need for Advertising
- Motivate the buyer
- Connect the consumer with the product and with the brand's values
- Develop the credibility and loyalty of customers
- Reinforce the identity of the company
- Differentiate yourself from the competition and
- Become unforgettable

Step #1: Define your strategy

How do you see your brand in the future?

Can you imagine your brand in 10 years? If you can do it, it is because you have a clear idea about how you want to define it, what values you want to associate it with, and in what way you want it to be linked to your audience. If you can do it all, your brand will probably be there ten years from now.

To define your Branding strategy, follow these tips:

1. Research

How do you know what values, emotions, and experiences you should associate with your brand? Investigate. Although you can decide how you want your brand to be perceived, it would be beneficial if you answer some questions before to guide your strategy:

1. Who are you? What are the elements that identify you and your competition?
2. What products or services do you offer? Define its main characteristics.
3. What are the core values that guide the actions of your company?
4. What are your mission and vision?
5. What does your company specialize in? What are you an expert in?
6. What is your target audience? Define their main demographic characteristics, psychographics.
7. What message do you want to convey?
8. Why should people choose your brand and not the competition?

You have already answered each of the questions. Just one more. Do you still see your brand in the future? If so, let's continue!

2. Know your target audience

What is the profile of the people who make up your target audience? At this point, you need to ask yourself what they want from your product or service, what they want. You must not disappoint them. After all, they are choosing you for a reason. It would be right for you to meet them.

The real reason why you should know your audience is that In this way, you will be able to offer a relevant value proposition and that that proposal arrives appropriately, through a message with which your audience feels identified, and that is meaningful to them.

3. Define your goals

You already know your brand's main characteristics and what your audience expects of you, their interests, tastes, and needs. It's time to set your brand goals. What do you want to achieve?

- ☐ Reach your audience with a clear message
- ☐ Achieve greater credibility
- ☐ Emotionally connect your audience with your brand
- ☐ Motivate consumers
- ☐ Achieve brand loyalty

Answering the following questions will help you define your goals:

- ☐ What do you want your brand to do for your company?
- ☐ What do you want people to know and say about your products or services?

4. Beyond the Brand: the promise

From the moment you make your brand known based on specific attributes, you make a promise. The promise that whatever happens, you will always be faithful to those values to which you associated it. And like anyone who commits, every time you stray from that path, your clients will be within their right to let you know.

Beyond the visual aspects, the brand is a concept, an idea. Something abstract that depends purely and exclusively on subjective elements, that is, on people's perception.

It is something extraordinary, since even if you sell the same product, consumers may prefer you instead of your competition; but at the same time somewhat risky.

Many times it doesn't matter what your intention was. People will perceive it according to their own experiences, history, values. And this may not agree with what you had proposed.

The promise implies that the brand transcends the product and, at the same time, becomes part of the consumer's life so that it always remains in their mind.

Developing a significant promise will allow your organization to connect with your customers emotionally and become ambassadors for your products.

After the design comes one of the most marathon tasks, you must communicate your brand's promise. Think about the message, the moment, and the supports through which you will make it reach your audience.

Here are some tips for creating a successful promise:

- **Be credible**: Don't make promises that you won't be able to keep.

- **Be emotional**: Connect emotionally with your audience. Make them feel identified with what your brand proposes.

- **Be relevant**: find out what your audience wants and is interested in.

- **Be consistent**: Between what the company is and what it claims to be. Promises, but delivers.

- **Be different**: Create a promise that makes you unique, causing you to be chosen and not your competition.

Example;

It could be said that FedEx, the American logistics company, knows well what branding is about. Since its inception, it has done everything possible to provide a differential value proposition, based purely and exclusively on its audience's needs and interests.

Thus, it has designed its brand proposal based on the idea that what they transport are not just packages and boxes. They are precious objects for their customers. Therefore, trust and credibility in the company are fundamental values to carry out its activities.

Their slogan "*We Understand*" makes it known that they know their customers' concerns and carry out shipments with the necessary responsibility and commitment because they know what these packages mean to them.

"*When you've achieved attributes like trust - which is essential to the business but doesn't make you fall in love with a brand - that's the moment when you start to think of your customer as a person and not as a number.*"

Kari Blanchard, Chief Strategy Officer, Future Brand New York office

Step #2: Logo

It is the heart of your brand.

Could you recognize the logos that appear in these images? What brands do they belong to? Indeed you have been able to recognize them and associate them with their companies. It has to do with the symbolic and representative power of the graphic.

As with these logos, through proper brand construction, it will be possible to make your brand logo iconic and unforgettable, which can be interpreted in itself, even without the rest of the visual elements of identity.

Remembrance + versatility + simplicity. These are the main qualities that you must gather. Here we give you some tips that will help design an effective logo for your Branding strategy. Take note!

- ***Keep it simple***

The simpler the design, the more quickly it will be understood and therefore remembered by your audience. The simplicity will also allow you to adapt your logo to different sizes, achieving greater versatility. The variation in the images' measures to adapt them to the other devices demands versatile logos in a multiscreen context.

☐ *Try it in black and white*

The use of colors is essential. The brand must be able to be perceived with all the senses. Colors convey different sensations and emotions in people, and their use contributes considerably to brand awareness.

However, a good logo has to achieve the same effect, even in black and white. Start designing it in these two colors only. Once the image is acquired, incorporate the colors with which you want to identify your brand.

☐ *Play with the hidden symbolism*

It is enjoyable to be able to play with the combination of words and images. It is the "Double Entendre" design technique. Look for something related to your brand identity and make sure that it is not entirely revealed at first glance.

Some examples of this technique can be LG and Amazon logos. Have you discovered the hidden message?

- *Make it unique and personal*

Any object can be incorporated into our logo and become the face of our brand. There are no limits to the imagination. However, make sure that it is consistent with your corporate identity.

What will make your brand unique is the fact of thinking about it to connect with your audience. Think about getting right to the mind of your customer. Connect with their emotions and interests.

If you have thought of an object that has already been used by other brands, be creative! Add a distinctive feature that makes it unique and unrepeatable (a fold at a vertex, a stroke.). The Apple logo, the apple with a bite, is an excellent example of this.

- *Vectorize it*

Thanks to programs such as Illustrator or CorelDraw, you can preserve the resolution of the image and prevent it from being pixelated when modifying its original size. It will make your job easier when adapting the logo to be used in any advertising medium (online or printed).

- *Use a professional designer*

Creating a logo seems to be a simple and even fun process. However, there are certain qualities that a logo must meet, and that often escape the eye of someone who is not specialized in it.

Remember! The logo is part of the first impression and the message that your company will convey. A professional can bring you new ideas and points of view and help you get the concept clearly and creatively, don't you think?

Creating a logo is not an easy task. We show you some mistakes that essential brands have made, seriously affecting their profits. Nobody is perfect!

> ➢ Google

Without a doubt, Google is one of the leading companies. Not only in the web market but also in the design of your branding. With what do you associate the combination of the colors green, red, blue, and yellow?

This brand has defied even the minimum design standards, escaping all parameters. Use serif letters and background shadows, rare elements. Another striking aspect is the use of doodles (cartoons and interactive) using its logo's letters to commemorate special events.

On the other hand, it has known, and very well, to build its brand architecture, providing an individual brand to each of its products, always protected by Google's visual identity. Anyone who sees your applications' logos can see with the naked eye that they belong to the company.

Still can't think of anything?

1. Look for inspiration on sites like Logopond.

2. Consult with friends and colleagues. One of the best ways to gather ideas is through brainstorming.

3. Some data to help you think:

    ☐ 33% of brands use the color blue for their logos

    ☐ 29% red

    ☐ 28% black or some color from the grayscale

    ☐ 13% yellow or gold

More interesting facts:

☐ 95% of brands use one or two colors

☐ 41% use only the text

☐ 9% do not name the company

The source of those data is PR Daily

Step #3: Naming

Your brand's name will identify it, differentiate it, define it, and connect it with its audience ... You have to think about it carefully! A name can lead your brand to devastating success or outrageous failure.

Why is it so important? The human mind works through categories that simplify its work. Each new knowledge that we acquire, we include it within one of those categories or create a new one. So, assigning a name to something will make it more easily stored in mind and therefore remembered.

Also, why do you think so many celebrities show business use stage names? The importance of choosing the appropriate name resides in that it conditions the perception that one has about what is named.

Defining the name that a brand will carry for the rest of its existence is not only a creative task. It is a purely strategic action, oriented according to the public's characteristics, the market, and the brand concepts you want to convey.

Do you want your brand to remain forever in the minds and hearts of consumers? We will give you a series of tips to simplify your work and take your brand to the top of mind.

1. Think about the web

In this case, the important thing is that if you have any ideas on how to name your brand, verify that the domain you want is available. On the other hand, it is not right to use a repeated name too much on the web, making it difficult to search.

2. Think simple

As you already know, the competition is great, and achieving a place in the consumer's mind is increasingly daunting. Even if it sounds too much, it must be creative, original, different, easy to pronounce and write, and finally, it must sound good.

3. Link it to your logo

Logo and name must be inseparable allies. One must describe the other, complement, and empower them. Seeks to achieve the perfect symbiosis between visual and linguistic memory.

4. Don't limit yourself

Try all the possible alternatives. Try in other languages, different concepts, ideas, and associations. Of course, if you choose words in another language, investigate if it does not negatively connotate other places.

5. Try it on Google AdWords

This tool will allow you to know the main trends regarding Internet searches. Thanks to this, you will know which are the most searched words in your sector, which have better positioning and a similar name.

6. Get everyone involved

The more people linked to the company participate in defining the name, the better. Each one will contribute their point of view and their knowledge about each area of the organization.

7. Think long term

Don't just think in a local context. Don't limit your expansion horizon. Avoid including a direct reference to your product and the place where you are, since if in the future everything turns out as you expected, you will need to make modifications.

8. Stand out

Observe your competition. What is your promise? What branding strategy do you use? Answering these questions will allow you to design a differentiating plan, pointing out where others do not.

There are several models for the syntactic construction of the brand name. These are some of them:

- ☐ *Descriptive*: The name is based on the description of your activity. Example: *Bangladesh Airlines*.

- ☐ *Neologism:* A new name is built based on two concepts. Example: Facebook (face + book).

- ***Abstract***: A name is created so far nonexistent. Example: Lego.

- Suggestive: There is talk of direct benefit. Example: *Social Tools* (social tools)

- ***Evocative***: You start from a known root and build a new concept. Example: Doppler (refers to the doppler effect) explained how an email (or wave) travels around the world in seconds and is read by thousands of people in different places, causing a response).

- ***Associative***: describes a concept. Example: *Lander* (to land). It is a tool to create landing pages or landing pages.

Google brand positioned in our minds and lives that have even created words from their name, such as goog-ling. Can you imagine making a brand from which a new language is developed?

If you intend to do the same, you must take into account the main elements of your brand:

- Brand image
- Business definition
- Characteristics of the product or service
- Target market
- Mission, vision, values, and beliefs

But ... how to achieve that much sought-after visual coherence so that your brand is remembered? Develop a Brand Manual. What is it about? We'll see.

Step #4: Your brand

It is the visual identity of your brand or the visible face of your company.

Both the logo and the name are part of the Corporate Identity, whose main objective is to visually represent your company's values through different elements, both physical and digital.

Can you imagine Coca Cola with a color other than red? Or Apple without the apple with its classic bite? This instant association that we make in our mind is related to how these brands have developed a coherent and consistent visual identity over time.

The challenge: to be unique or to be nothing

If you intend to do the same, you must take into account the main elements of your brand:

- ☐ Brand image
- ☐ Business definition
- ☐ Characteristics of the product or service
- ☐ Target market
- ☐ Mission, vision, values, and beliefs

But ... how to achieve that much sought-after visual coherence so that your brand is remembered? Develop a Brand Manual. What is it about? We'll see.

The Brand Manual

It is a guide that details the primary standards and guidelines intended to guide the different ways in which the brand and logo should be applied to the other media, both internal and external.

This normative manual will include every one of the technical specifications (shape, colors, sizes, typography.) and aesthetics related to the design of all physical or digital corporate materials: posters, stationery, emails.

There will appear each of the opportunities in which they should be used and in what way. Also, the actions that are prohibited regarding the graphic use of the brand will be defined.

What is the use of investing time, effort, and money if later, the logo and the name are not going to be publicized in the way they were designed? Far from trying to limit the designer's work, it. The main objective is to stimulate their creativity by clarifying how the company aspires to convey its brand identity.

The aspects that are commonly developed in it include:

- The logo and its distinctive features
- The official font of the brand
- The communicational tone of it
- The palette of the most representative colors
- Tips and essential points to take into account when designing the different supports

There are simple manuals where only colors, sizes, and fonts are specified and manuals of more than 1,000 pages where each of the elements and the specific application case is detailed.

The real importance of having a consistent visual identity lies in:

- Increase recognition of the company
- Increase visibility

- ☐ Develop trust on the part of employees
- ☐ Save costs by standardization
- ☐ Achieve homogeneity of criteria when applying the brand

Once your brand strategy has been wholly designed: name, logo, and visual identity in general, it only remains to communicate that brand, and perhaps the most critical challenge of all: to position it in people's minds. Can you?

Step #5: Brand positioning

Brand positioning is to occupy a place in the mind of people.

Each company that develops a Branding strategy does so to occupy a privileged place in its audience's mind. That is, to position it. It implies differentiating it from its competition in the consumer's mind, designing a differentiated place to place its image and its products/services by enhancing its distinctive characteristics.

Positioning a brand has to do with becoming one of the benchmarks in your market sector. Being one of the main alternatives, if not the only one in which the consumer deposits their trust and money. His goal is to make him able to distinguish the qualities of your company from those that your competition provides and make them prefer yours.

Suppose you mentioned a soft drink brand, a software development brand, and an automobile brand. Surely your answer would be within what the average person imagines. Coincidence? Of course not. Is that the brands that came to your mind, have done excellent management of branding and positioning?

Do you want to know how to position your brand among the first in the market? Follow these tips:

1. Whom are you refer to?

Another question: how to position yourself in the mind of someone you don't know? If you do not see what interests him and what he hates, how do you plan to reach one of the first positions in his mind? Define your audience variable by variable. A good technique would be to ask what attributes they consider relevant.

2. What characteristics does your market have?

Answer the following questions and get a more precise notion:

- What are the attributes of the product or service to which your target reacts favorably?

- Who are your competitors, and what is their positioning strategy?

- How are the different competing brands perceived these distinctive features?

- What would be the best marketing and communication mix to position yourself effectively in your target mind?

- What resources do you have to develop a campaign that allows you to position your brand?

3. Define your positioning strategy

According to the information you have managed to obtain, you will be ready to decide which is the most effective strategy.

- **By differential advantage**

If the products or services you sell are unique in the market due to some particular characteristics, you can use this as an element on which to build your brand.

Apple is an expert in "*Think Different.*"

Since its inception, it has made a difference in each of its products:

Its design will continue through its innovation until it reaches its brand's construction, history, and promise: to challenge even reality itself to offer something innovative, different, and focused on providing an excellent user experience.

- **By price**

One way to differentiate yourself is by appealing to what most customers are looking for: prices. Whether due to low prices or high prices, in both cases, it is a positioning strategy.

"Always low prices" and "Save money, live better" are clear examples of the differential advantage that Walmart is aiming for. Selling your products at low prices is your promise and your way of differentiating yourself at the same time.

Instead, Ferrari has built a brand strategy based on exclusivity. How many people can access one of your cars? Designing products almost to order, with practically unique qualities, together with a pricing strategy based on quality and exclusivity, leads to position the brand in a top of mind (first positions in people's minds).

- **By type of competition**

When the market is saturated, the competition is intense and abundant. The only option is to differentiate. Although it may seem complicated, having an in-depth understanding of your competition's brand strategy will help you define yours.

Still don't know how? Well, we offer you two alternatives that will allow you to position your brand about your competition:

☐ *Position yourself as the opposite*

Even when your company sells the same product as others, there are many ways to make a difference. You may well target another audience or a particular niche.

You can differentiate yourself based on your visual identity or do it based on the promise you make to your audience, showing that yours is diametrically opposite.

Let's take an example;

NIKE AND ADIDAS

Two companies are dedicated to the sale of footwear and sportswear. When it comes to the product, there is no apparent difference that makes a person choose one over another. The difference lies in another aspect: its promise.

NIKE's strategy aims at competitiveness, passion for sport, self-confidence to excel, while at the same time placing individualism as a primary value to achieve our goals. Their motto "Just do it" contains a motivating message, designed to encourage everyone to do what they want to do, without thinking about the result.

Meanwhile, ADIDAS aims to enjoy the passion for a hobby, regardless of whether that hobby is a sport. Its motto "Adidas is all in" refers to the brand's presence in different areas: sporting, cultural, lifestyle, music, and fashion.

Thus, the brand representatives from soccer star like Lionel Messi and David Beckham, through great NBA players like Derrick Rose, pop icons like Kety Perry.

The message conveyed in his commercial is clear: "*We give everything and go for more. Without hesitation, without holding back, without giving up. From the field to the catwalk, from the stadium to the street. Whatever the challenge, we always play it the same way: our hearts and as a team. United by passion. We go all in.*"

These strategies show how two brands engaged in the same activity and even aim at the same target can differentiate themselves from the construction of their brand and the promise they hold.

- ***Position yourself as the challenger***

It's never easy to be second. But ranking second also has its advantages: it allows you to challenge the first. How? Aim to associate your brand with totally different attributes or offer alternative products. You can also match your Marketing mix to improve the points where your competition is weak or failing.

The most exhibited example in the fascinating world of branding is Coca Cola and its eternal competition: Pepsi. The latter has always been the second brand positioned in the soft drink market. However, far from resigning itself to occupying this place and not overcoming its rival, it decided to adopt the strategy of positioning itself as a challenger.

To challenge its opponent, in the late 1970s, Pepsi launched a global campaign called "The Pepsi Challenge." The objective was to demonstrate, which was the preferred taste of consumers.

To do this, they set up stands in the main shopping centers of the world, with two identical glasses, without identification, one contained Coca Cola and the other Pepsi, people had to take a sip from the two glasses and choose the one they liked the most. The result? Most picked the glass with Pepsi.

- *Multiple positioning*

According to each particular brand, some large companies in terms of their structure and that have multiple brands will use each positioning strategy based on the analysis of their market, product characteristics, target audience, and promise, among many other variables.

Once you have decided what your positioning strategy will be, it will be time to think about what actions you will put into practice to make your audience fall in love and get them always to choose you. Ready to plan your conquest strategy?

Step #6: Brand loyalty

Make them love your brand.

The reality is that we all seek to be loved and faithful to us. Brands too! Each company builds a bond with its audiences, especially with its customers.

This emotional bond is generated from the experiences, feelings, and perceptions generated in each contact. Depending on the degree to which consumers engage with your brand, it will be the loyalty they develop towards it.

Is it easy to achieve loyal consumers? The answer: NO. Economic crises, price variations, intense competition, among other factors, make it almost impossible to achieve the long-awaited consumer loyalty.

Indeed you have a product that you buy regularly but only if it belongs to a particular brand or company. Good for it! Because this is achieving brand loyalty. It is to accomplish the repeated purchase of a product or service due to the perceived value, trust, and bond generated between the client-company.

The objective of your strategy should be: to turn your clients into ambassadors of your brand. To do this, achieving the maximum degree of satisfaction about your products and increasing the perception of added value that you contribute to their consumer experiences will be essential ingredients in the recipe for your branding's success.

Loyalty differs from positioning in the sense that it can be observed from an attitude (built based on attributes that a consumer perceives and values of a brand) and from a behavior (measurable through a commitment to the company, intention, execution, or repurchase).

Why have loyal customers?

It may be that the question is redundant, but it is essential that you know that developing consumer loyalty towards your brand has a triple benefit for your company.

Increase your income: The higher the perceived value and satisfaction, the greater the loyalty and repeat purchases. Your payment will increase while you develop a more robust and lasting relationship with your customers.

Lower sensitivity to price: As a result of a higher level of involvement, your customers will develop less sensitivity to your product or service price changes.

More recommendations, more word of mouth: As a customer increases their degree of satisfaction and loyalty with your company, they will recommend it. And not only to your group of belonging, but social networks can also achieve a significant role in this regard.

How to achieve the loyalty of your customers?

The study "Brand Keys Loyalty Leaders 2011,[2]" carried out by Forbes magazine, showed that the brands that enjoy the most loyalty are those that have a real influence on people's daily lives. Think about how you can be part of the everyday life of your clients!

In the Forbes list, the companies with the highest consumer loyalty were: Amazon, Apple, Facebook, Samsung, Zappos, Hyundai, and Kindle, everyday brands that are not necessarily accessible.

Authentic loyalty is achieved through constant communication that shows the product and its honest and human face.

The importance of building a trusted brand is that it generates an emotional response in consumers. The secret to getting them to love your brand lies in continually adding value in each of your business's critical areas.

There are different phases in loyalty development that your potential customers go through. Knowing them will help plan actions to increase loyalty to your brand, depending on the stage in which they are.

---

[2] https://www.forbes.com/sites/marketshare/2011/09/13/top-100-loyalty-leaders-for-2011/

- *Unawareness*

At this stage, your potential customers cannot differentiate your products or services from those of your competition. You are in real trouble! One of the reasons may be a lousy brand positioning, that is, that you have made a mistake in any of the steps to design your Branding strategy.

- *Recognition*

Good news! You are already present in the mind of your audience. When making the purchase decision, your products are taken into account by them, even if they finally choose the competition's product or service.

- *Preference*

Product of a positive experience, consumers decide to choose your products over those of the competition. Of course, this is not final but can be modified as new products and competitors emerge.

- *Loyalty*

It is the ideal phase! Your customers choose your brand, even after having had problems with it or even in circumstances where a competitor's product could be functionally superior.

If you have managed to reach this phase, you already enjoy a close bond with your consumers, and they are involved with your brand. Excellent work!

Here we leave you five tips that will make your brand have originality, creativity but above all, the love necessary to attract your target.

1. Innovation to excel

Bring out the extraordinary. Always look for an extra that makes a difference. A brand sells more for the idea it represents than for the product.

2. Generate quality content

To fall in love and propose, you must connect with the lifestyle of each of your clients. The content must be 100% related to the client's needs.

3. Customize each experience

It is the extra that will make customers feel unique. You must use emotions. Never forget that the most loyal customers have to feel rewarded and, in some way, loved. It is achieved through discounts, but it must be ensured that the brand-client relationship is not broken for anything.

4. Maintain a dialogue

The client will feel part of the brand when it is taken into account and communication is established.

5. Measure actions

It will check if each of your strategies works and will allow you to improve your results more and more. Deliver promptly, not just promise to sell.

Chapter 4

Content Marketing

Content marketing is a marketing technique for creating and distributing relevant and valuable content to attract, acquire, and attract the attention of a well-defined target audience to encourage them to be future customers.

Most users think that content marketing is based solely on creating content. They are not misguided. The problem is that creating content does not have to be content marketing.

The four challenges of Content Marketing

1. Produce enough content
2. Produce good content
3. Get budget
4. Variety of content

Why do content marketing?

- Improve your brand image. If you give your users useful and personalized content, you will improve your reputation and visibility.

- It allows you to generate direct and close relationships with your users, naturally and openly.

- It is cheaper and more profitable.

- Improve your search engine rankings.

- It inevitably makes you think about your users, with the myriad of advantages that this entails.

You have endless options to promote your content. Do not get carried away by the easy: Facebook and Twitter and little else, Although they have their advantages too. The idea is to try new means. Innovate, try new things. Have you never uploaded a presentation to SlideShare? It is another means of attracting traffic and leads. What are you waiting for?

Prepare a good content plan with its corresponding editorial calendar to know in advance what you should do, when, how, where, and why. Only then will all this be successful.

Content Inbound Marketing

This theory, put forward by content marketing specialists, is based on the so-called Consumer Journey, used as Inbound Marketing. Which is shown in the following image:

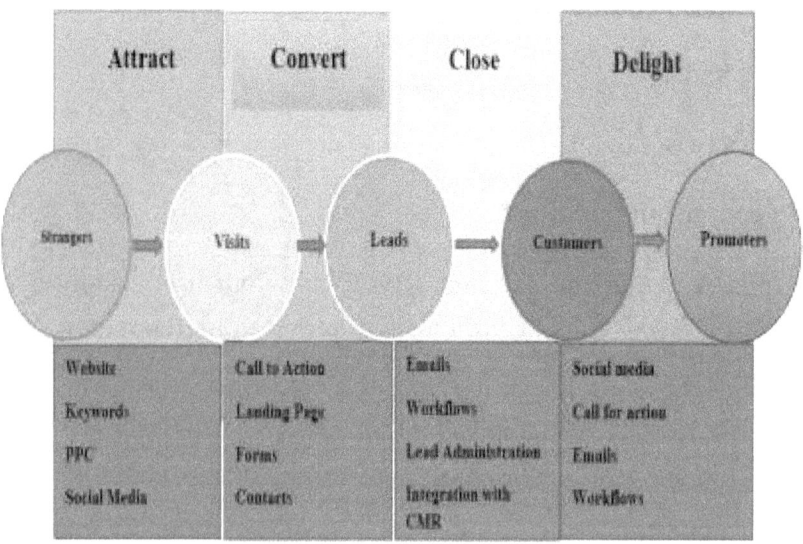

The main objective of the Inbound Marketing methodology is to attract the people defined as the target audience, convert them into customers, and retain them so that they love the brand and promote it, thus getting more customers naturally and reliably.

In each of the stages of this methodology (attract, convert, close, and delight), it is necessary to serve people the right content to satisfy their information needs about the product or service they are interested in purchasing. That's where the Content Inbound Marketing Funnel comes in.

The Content Inbound Marketing ensures that each of the online content pieces is what users expect to find, thus enhancing each website's search engine positioning campaigns.

Structure of the Content Marketing Funnel

The first step towards success in an SEO strategy after defining the target audience's main characteristics is keyword research. At this time, we have an approach to what digital content should be developed for every stage of the consumer journey. The structure of the funnel is as follows:

Content   **Marketing**   **Funnel**

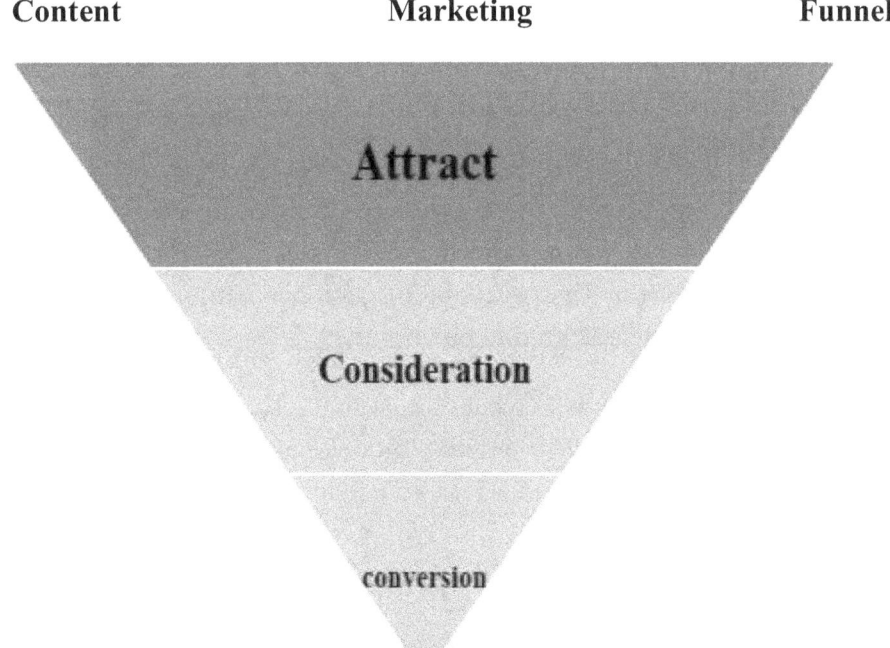

Attract

Here we educate potential customers. We help them understand the problems they face with the products or services they are trying to acquire, the situations of use, examples, and other users' experiences. The objective is to demonstrate the credibility of the brand.

Some tools for SEO content creation are the following:

- Blog posts
- Informative articles about the industry and products in general
- Webinars or videos on the company's channels
- Complete guides on the operation, applications, and more
- Frequently asked questions from users
- Press releases
- Opinions of influencers

Consideration

In this part, the person already knows their real need and the solutions they obtain when acquiring the product or service they are looking for. It is the first success of any generation of content-oriented to natural search engine positioning.

The user already knows what he wants. He concentrates on determining which of all the brands, models, and prices is the most convenient for his investment. Here you should create content pieces such as:

- Study cases
- Technical information and characteristics of the products

- Demonstration of the use of the products through videos
- User guides and manuals
- References from other clients

At this stage of the content marketing strategy, the objective is to convince people that our brand is the one they need. Remember that at this time, the user already knows what he wants. He only has to decide between the market options for the same product or service.

Conversion

What all SEO positioning planning seeks is conversion. A conversion is an action that the user must perform, depending on the business objective. It can be a sale, a download. The important thing here is to stimulate the leads, or future clients, to make the final decision in a subtle yet effective way.

The types of content that best benefit from this situation are:

- Comments from other users
- Happy buyers testimonials
- Possibility of accessing a demo version (in the case of online services)
- Free consultation channels, pre, and post-sale
- Performance guarantees

Creation of high-quality SEO content

The relationship between a search engine optimization strategy and the content marketing funnel is a symbiosis. We cannot think about an SEO campaign's success without defining a target audience, creating appropriate content for each decision stage, and providing a compelling call to action, that is, converting leads or prospects into customers.

Some aspects to take into account when creating quality content:

- **Understanding the audience**: use the language of the users. It will result in choosing the right keywords and creating content that meets the target audience's needs.

- **Stay focused**: help readers complete a specific task. Each piece of content should focus on a single topic.

- **Call to action**: the content must close with a clear call to action. Something that tells the user to do more than just read an article, or watch a video.

Knowing the target audience is essential to create unique, attractive content, which is the star of any SEO positioning strategy.

There are free SEO tools to guide you through the process.

1-Ubersuggest

It is a free keyword matching tool, essential for carrying out SEM or SEO campaigns. The platform can quickly suggest various keyword combinations, depending on the keyword you entered in the search engine.

It is beneficial because it will allow you to work on content in the long tail through the synonyms of these keywords that you have entered.

It is currently owned by Neil Patel, one of the biggest names in Digital Marketing worldwide. After acquiring Ubersuggest, Neil Patel has created a potent tool capable of combining the best of Google Keyword Planner with Google Suggest, adding and improving the following functions:

- Refinement and more volume suggested keywords
- Availability of CPC (cost per click), competition, and search volume
- Advanced filtering capabilities
- Ability to export data in CVS

2-SEMRush

The SEMRush tool is used mainly to analyze data related to SEO, that is, web positioning, and develop strategies to get backlinks to a website or build advertising.

It is also beneficial to detect and analyze the competition. For example, knowing the keywords they use to position themselves and looking for new keywords to attack our competition by looking for a different market niche that they have not used can attract more public.

If that is the country your positioning is focused on, Spain's database is much more complete in SEMRush.

SEMrush provides you with the following information about your direct competitors:

- Level of competition
- Common keywords
- The keywords that a competitor has in the search engine
- Organic traffic from a competitor
- Payment keywords and traffic price

3- Answer the Public

It is a free tool that allows us to collect information about a specific key term and respond to users. A keyword will show us all the questions, searches, and related suggestions that users make on the Internet.

Created by Coverage Book, this tool will allow you to know all the questions your users ask themselves when inserting that specific term in the search engine. It is as simple as indicating the keyword to be tracked, setting the country and language, and returning a complete result of the searches made in search engines on that specific keyword and multiple variants. All this information will be summarized in tables, arranged alphabetically.

You can read this article: [8 SEO Tools to Help Guide your Content Strategy](#) if you want to know more about the SEO tools.

Chapter 5

Facebook Marketing

Marketing on Facebook is the answer to the communication you wanted with your audiences.

You may already know that Facebook is the number one social media platform that most people use. The statistics show that.

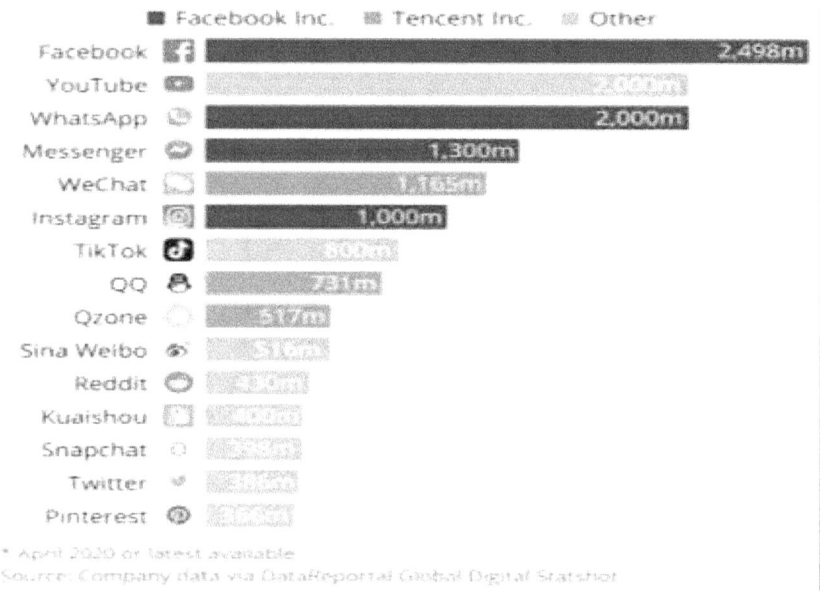

And it's not just Facebook either... according to Similar Web, all of the big platforms get tons of traffic:

- LinkedIn – 917 million visitors a month

- Twitter – 3.62 billion visitors a month

- YouTube – 22.77 billion visitors a month

- Pinterest – 722 million visitors a month

- Instagram – 2.86 billion visitors a month

Facebook Statistics

Facebook continues to dominate social media platforms. It is the most used platform among both marketers and consumers, according to the Sprout Social 2019 Index. Here are some impressive social media statistics related to Facebook:

- 89% of marketers use Facebook in their brand marketing efforts

- 83% of surveyed consumers use the platform

- 66% say they Like or Follow a brand on the platform

- By the third quarter of 2019, the platform had attracted 2.5 million monthly active users

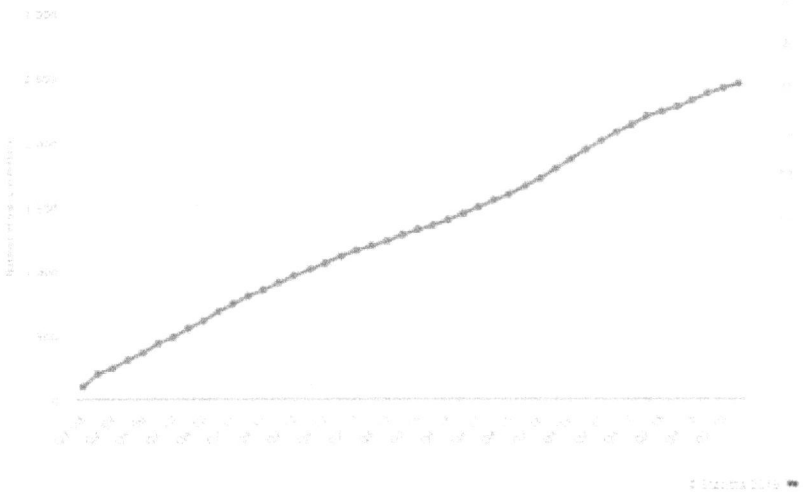

- Live video is becoming a vital tool for social marketers, and 42% of them have already developed a strategy for Facebook Live

- From posting a median of 0.97 posts per day, brands are seeing a median engagement rate of 0.09% on the platform across all industries

- Along with its growing user base, the platform also sees an increase in revenue. It generated $17.65 billion in total revenue in the third quarter of 2019

- Out of this, a majority came from advertising. It isn't too surprising considering how Facebook had over 7 million advertisers during Q3 of 2019

- Facebook use among U.S. marketers is slightly increasing from 86.3% in 2018 to 86.8% in 2019. This number will likely reach 87.1% in 2020

After seeing all that information about Facebook marketing, if you are looking for the most effective Facebook marketing strategies, this chapter is a must-read.

Customer interaction

Increasing your interactions on Facebook is not impossible. But first, answer these questions. Have you noticed that FB changes its algorithm more often lately? Did you know that when the algorithm is updated, the rules of the game change for everyone? Some benefit more than others, and many talks about inbound marketing, content marketing, storytelling, but very few tell you precisely what you should do to generate engagement.

1.- Analyze your audience

Many people think that analyzing the public is to know more women than men or vice versa. The analysis should go much deeper than that. To begin with, do you know who your target audience is? Perhaps your primary audience is between 18 and 24 years old. If your posts are jokes or topics related to the '70s or '80s, there will be no commitment because they don't understand what you're talking about.

You can also give yourself the opportunity that the audience you want to attract is between the ages of 13 and 19 for the products you offer; However, by the design line that you follow, you are capturing people from 34 to 42 who could be the parents or adult relatives of your target audience, and you are not directing the communication towards them. They are specific things that many brands do not take into account when publishing. If you want to find this information, you can easily find it on your Facebook page, click on statistics and then in the information list on the left, click on People, and you will find the information you need to improve your interactions on Facebook with your real audience.

2.- Talk about the achievements and important dates of the company

Not everything in social networks is sales. Some brands have become "Loved Brands" because they always talk about real stories; they always acted very entrepreneurially and gave something to talk about. Social networks serve to share varied, fun, emotional content, but it is also necessary that the users of your products and followers can see the personality behind the brand, that humanizes it, makes it real, and brings it closer to the public that could become your clientele, followers or users. Talk about the workers of the month, congratulate them on their birthdays (this way you motivate them and show them how special they are to your company), talk about how the company started in numbers and now the great team they form, talk warmly about your collaborators and also mention some of his achievements. Many of their stories and yours could serve as inspiration for the audience.

3.- Start your posts creatively

There is much difference in starting a position like: Buy This Cream And Look Better Than A Title Like Lose Weight In 12 Days Start Today! (link to blog) Always try to start your posts positively. Starting with negatives can be counterproductive and can make your audience lose interest in what you post. Some GIFs tend to be very elementary, but they can go viral only if you think strategically before posting with an excellent caption.

4.- From time to time, ASK QUESTIONS

Everything you share is reasonable offers or information. It is very flattering to include questions so that the public can give their point of view and you can quickly make a decision about it. Sometimes ideas run out due to stress and every day. Asking your audience what they would like you to share can be very important because they can give you incredible ideas. Try it!

5.- Share eye-catching photos and videos with a fair resolution

Always before publishing, ask yourself, would I share this post? Would you answer or tag someone? It is not recommended to use Google photos unless they are released by the author (CC0). You can find this type of content on Pixabay and many other pages.

SEO

Positioning in search engines is not a process exclusively linked to Google. On the contrary, when brands optimize content, they must do so on all their online platforms, and this includes the Fan Pages of their social media accounts, where Facebook plays a leading role. How to do it? Follow the tips below:

1. Reserve the best URL for your brand

Facebook allows us to put a "custom" URL. This URL should not only respond to a word-of-mouth criterion "*https://www.facebook.com/MyCompanyName*" as it plays a crucial role in SEO.

If you haven't claimed this URL as a business yet, do so! You will need at least 25 likes to reserve it. The URL should be very similar to the name of your company.

Forget the dashes and underscores in the URL. Facebook doesn't allow it. It significantly limits the variety of typical SEO tricks that we can apply. Think it over before making your decision. Facebook won't let you change it later.

2. Your company/brand name is critical

It may seem obvious but let's remember that the name you refer to your brand on the Facebook page is crucial! You have to make it as easy as possible for your customers to find you. They will not look for your brand in more than one or two different ways. If your name is difficult to remember or write, it will be difficult for them to find you. Does the Schweppes case sound familiar to you? Even today, it is still a complicated name!

Fortunately, we have a small margin of maneuver where we can include some "keywords" related to our brand. Stay away from your brand as much as possible.

3. Fill in all the information you can

Make it as easy as possible for your clients to find you. Facebook provides us with three fields to describe our business, use them all correctly and in detail.

In "Profile> Basic information," we must edit all the fields: The "Information" field is the smallest; it is conceivable that it serves to include the slogan of the brand or company. In "Description" and "Company profile," they allow you to have more information. Write a description in such a way that it includes almost all the keywords that define your company but forms easy-to-read sentences. It is not as easy as it looks

Complete the rest of the fields with real information and channels regularly reviewed (it seems obvious, but there are thousands of emails that go directly to the bottom of the sea where no one will ever read them).

4. Link it

Do not forget that the Google PageRank algorithm is based on the number of links. Nothing can be better for your fan page than having more links, the better as long as they are valid links. Link from the official page of the brand/company to the Facebook page.

Putting links from the official page to the Facebook page will generate traffic and also improve your positioning. Putting links in the opposite direction, no, Facebook always includes "unfollow," so put links that provide content for your users.

Free Promotion

How to promote my business on Facebook for Free? Let's start some options for you to promote your business for free on your Facebook. Let's get started!

Option #1: Join Facebook groups

Facebook groups, unlike Fan Pages, allow users to debate, share their content.

An excellent way to publicize your business is to belong to these but related to what you offer.

You can share and interact with people with your client's profile, and when you already have a good relationship, you go and show your business, for example, tech groups where users talk about the latest phone equipment, computers. You can interact with them and, at any time, present your software development business or cell phone sales (for example).

Option #2: Exchange promotion

It could also be a very significant payment method, but you can also take advantage of it for free (for something it is an answer to how to promote my business on Facebook for free).

Let's suppose you have a FanPage with followers, and other people have it too.

However, you may be interested in reaching their audience and reaching yours to do a kind of barter. You promote their business or FanPage, and they do the same with you.

As always, you have to pay close attention to the subject where you will be promoted.

Go out of the free. It would be more comfortable. It is a matter of locating FanPages with good visits and your theme to pay because they promote you. But since you don't have money now, you are going to start the exchange.

Option #3: Befriend people with your account profile

In this case, we forget a bit about the FanPage. You have to create your ordinary Facebook account, but make friends with people who may be interested in your business.

For this, you should spend a little time adding the right people. It is a good idea to consider those who follow FanPage or belong to groups with themes similar to yours and add it ...

That is, you go to a FanPage that talks about beauty, and the people who follow them add it as your friend (in case you have a beauty salon).

The next step is to lead an ordinary life on Facebook. It is forbidden to go crazy and do SPAM! But you do have to identify yourself as someone who knows about beauty (following the same example), so share tips, images related to your sector.

Then you can take advantage and promote yourself, present your business, and from time to time, share your FanPage or whatever is related to your business.

The advantage of doing this over the FanPage is that they do not have to follow or like you. You are the one who chooses who will be able to see your publications. Yes, I know! The person is who agrees to be your friend, but this is not difficult. Almost all people accept the requests that come to them unless they look suspicious or dangerous.

Option #4: Direct promotion Be very careful

Do you know what a perfect but dangerous answer to how to promote my business on Facebook is? Direct promotion.

I ask that if you do this, be very careful. I would say too much! I would not like you to end up doing SPAM.

If the previous idea seems a bit long because you have to add people, they have an everyday life on Facebook and then promote yourself ... I have a faster solution.

You will do the same as in the previous space, but you will save the everyday life on Facebook. In other words, you will go to Facebook groups, FanPage, and you will add people ...

Once they accept you, you politely send them a private message presenting your business and yourself as a person. If you have a

FanPage, blog, or any other site to show more confidence and credibility, it is not wrong that you mention it.

Many will ignore you, but I assure you that they will be hooked if you push yourself the right amount. Here the important thing is three things:

- **That they accept the request** and then send the message if it is not very likely that the recipient will not even notice it because Facebook takes them to a hidden folder to avoid SPAM. Something that does not happen when we are friends!

- **Vary the messages**, so Facebook will not bother you saying that you are doing SPAM, so I recommend you act naturally.

- **Make an effort to see the result**. Do not think that you will have very noticeable results if you only send a daily email. Take your time and dedicate yourself to this task for a long time.

And if many ignore you, don't worry, especially if it is a local business because I'm sure that person will remember you when you walk around your town.

It is like TV commercials, many "Ignore" it, yet they know of its existence. And what matters to us is that they know of your presence, and later when they need you, they will remember you.

Responding To Problems

- *Be proactive and respond to the comments they leave you*

95% of the brands on Facebook leave this point very neglected. Facebook, like Twitter, is a perfect customer service channel. By responding to comments and questions quickly, users will see your engagement with them. It takes you no more than a minute, and it does a lot for you because it's a straightforward way to increase engagement and build lasting relationships with your fans.

Like any analysis of your target market, you will need to know its characteristics in-depth. What interests them, what they prefer to avoid, what they want and requires, their main problems, and what topics they have fun with.

Facebook is characterized by being a social network used mainly by middle-aged people. 61% of its users are under 35 years old. Of which 70% are about women who - believe it or not - publish 62% of the total content, according to a study by the Pew Research Center.

Another fact that will catch your attention and make you focus your efforts on this social network is that according to a BI Intelligence investigation[3], 73% of its users earn more than $ 75,000 annually, beating any other system by more than one 50% in income.

If your target audience has these characteristics, don't hesitate any longer! Facebook is the place to be.

☐ *Monitor relevant conversations*

At this point, there are two aspects that you should keep in mind. First, the idea that human beings guide their behavior based on emotions and therefore their decisions - especially those related to purchases - will be affected by the opinions of other people, family, and friends to a greater extent.

Second, constant monitoring of conversations between members of your community, as well as people outside of it and even from other social networks, will allow you to: learn about topics of interest to your audience, detect potential conflicts for your brand, Get to know

---

[3] https://www.insiderintelligence.com/bii/

your target audience in-depth, identify new markets and opportunities for your products.

Knowing what is being discussed on social networks will be very beneficial to raise your strategies. Do you know what the most significant advantage of doing it is? Be one step ahead of your competition, and increase engagement with your community in an exponential way.

Beating Your Competition

Who is your competition in social networks?

Competition in social networks are all those accounts with the same or similar content to yours, so they go beyond the businesses you fight in products or services, and the radius increases to those websites, brands, or media that talk about the same as you on social networks.

A recommended action to do before or during the management of a brand in social networks is to know what your competition is doing to draw up a strategy that brings you closer to meeting your objectives.

Below, a series of freeways you can spy on your competition on Facebook to beat them.

1-Pages under observation

Through the statistics of your fan page, you have the option of adding other pages in observation with which you can compare yourself in performance and publications, the metrics that mark you are:

- Total likes
- Increase in likes compared to last week
- Number of posts for the week

- Number of interactions for the week

It gives you data with which you can see if you have a worse or better evolution according to those KPIs, but you have to take them with care since community volume is a factor that alters a lot. If you have a 1,000-fan page, you may have worse numbers than a 20,000-fan page with increasing likes and interactions.

2-Barometer by AgoraPulse

With this tool, you can compare your fan page with others with a similar community volume. You can measure, among others:

- Scope
- Reach rate
- Interaction rate
- CTR
- Feedback

You have to take it carefully since the community margins with which it works are complete, and it is also analyzing pages from all over the world and from different sectors, essential factors that can significantly vary your metrics.

More inspiration than reference.

It is freemium. With the free part, you can see essential aspects to be able to develop the analysis.

3-Metricool

It is one of the necessary tools with which we work at Wanatop within the Social Department, among others, thanks to the data it gives us to compare ourselves with the competition on Facebook and Instagram.

Within this, it creates a classification in which you can compare:

- "Like" the page
- Publications
- Reactions
- Comments
- Shared
- Engagement

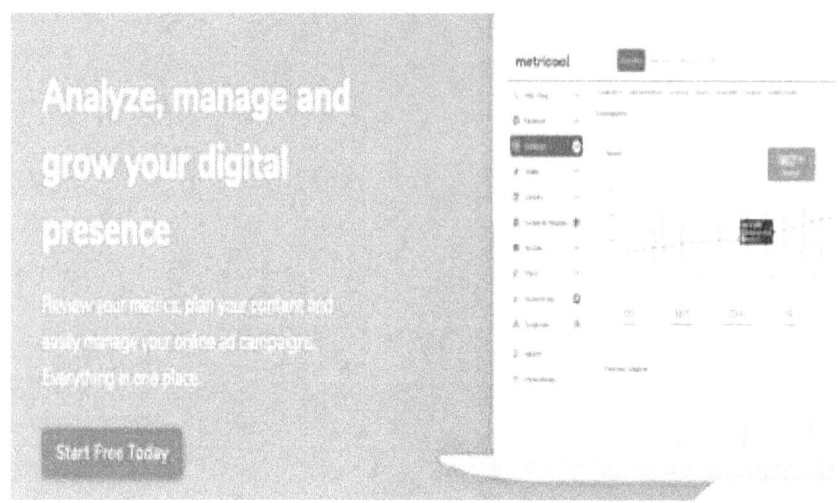

If you also add your page to this classification, you will see what position you are in. It is advisable to take engagement as a reference.

Also, it shows you graphs of community evolution and interactions, beneficial to detect campaigns or actions.

4-Audience Insights

Also known as "Audience Statistics."

It is a tool that you can access through Facebook Ads in which you have data at the demographic level, a fan of other pages, place, and activity, of specific interest.

If Facebook considers your competition as an interest, you can see what their fans are like.

For this, there is no clear barometer by which we can know if a page is an interest at the level of segmentation in advertising. For example, pages with 50,000 fans who are interested and others with the same volume are not.

You can also use it for the pages you are managing to see if you have a quality community based on other fan pages you like if they fall within the buyer persona you are looking for.

5-Announcement Library

It is a tool that Facebook had opened within its strategic line of transparency, by which we can see the ads that a Facebook page has active and other data such as when it was created or the history of name changes.

What can you analyze? All this:

- Active ads by countries.
- Creatives: people appear, the product alone, the combination of both ...
- Formats: video, image, carousel ...
- Communication style: the copy you use, how you speak to the user, use, or not of emojis ...
- Landing pages: home, category, product, landing ...
- Locations in which they appear: Instagram news, Facebook news, Instagram Stories ...
- UTMs: Do you follow any tracking? Spy utms that are in the URLs to see if there is any clue of the public, campaign, objective

That is pure gold. You can access it from here.

6-Facebook Pixel

If a fan page is investing in advertising on Facebook by sending traffic to a website, the most normal thing is that that website has implemented the Facebook Pixel to track user activity and work with remarketing or public lists similar or make conversion campaigns.

To detect if the Facebook Pixel is on, install the Facebook Pixel Helper extension in Google Chrome, informing you if the code is implemented and the different events it works with. In this way, you can know if it has the Pixel at a basic level of attracting visits or more advanced with events of lead, purchase, add to cart, or other options.

As you can see, there are different ways to analyze other brands on Facebook from the outside, and without the need to invest in tools. Bringing them all together, you will be able to get an idea of how your competition is working on this social network to inspire you and beat them.

Facebook Ads

To compete, at least on Facebook, you will have to pay. This situation, known sector as "pay to play," has its origin in the changes in the Facebook algorithm that Mark Zuckerberg already announced under the excuse of pursuing a greater connection with our Facebook friendships and that have been happening since then.

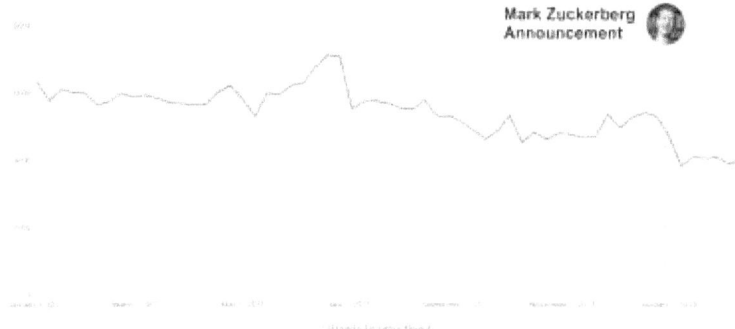

With that said, get to the point! The first thing you should know to get down to work is that Facebook Ads are composed and configured in three parts:

- Campaign
- Ad Set
- Ads or advertisements

Campaign

A Facebook campaign is like a matryoshka. Each element that you configure encompasses the following to advance from decisions that affect all parties to decisions that only include one of them.

In this case, the campaign is an excellent container for everything that will come after it, so you will have to decide your objective and how you want to pay.

- *goals*

You can see everything you can achieve with your Facebook ads packaged in three main objectives related to the conversion funnel in this image.

Awareness: if you want your content to have more notoriety, Facebook allows you to choose that your ads are distributed to the more people, the better (reach), or to the people who are more likely to remember them (Brand Awareness). Quantity vs. Quality. In this case, what you will pay for is per thousand impressions, called CPM (cost per thousand).

Consideration: one step further, since what the objectives of consideration are pursuing is greater involvement on the part of the user: go to your page (traffic), get some type of interaction, going from likes and comments to fans (engagement), download your app, consume your videos in a greater or lesser measure of time, get your data (lead generation) or establish a conversation (messages). Based on your choice, you will pay per click (CPC), per interaction (CPI), per view (CPV).

Conversion: It is to get direct conversions from Facebook. It will be essential that you have the corresponding pixel installed on your page.

As we said, in this step, you will also decide how to pay. If in advance, make sure that you will achieve fixed objectives with your investment in advance, "reserving" the audience to impact (what is known as reach and frequency) or by bidding.

If you have a low budget (under which we will follow the rest of the instructions), Reach, and Frequency will be less accessible since the costs are high. However, with the bid format, you can decide what price you want to compete to impact an audience.

Along with two other factors related to the probability that your ad will like the selected audience, if your bid is higher than that of the rest of the accounts bidding to impact the same user segmentation, Facebook will distribute your ads. If it is not, it will wait for the price to drop to do so. That is why you will not know if you will achieve your target figures in advance, and you will have to work based on estimates.

Ad Set

Let's assume that our goal is to drive traffic to a blog. We will have selected this option in the campaign settings, and now it is time to make the decisions related to the ad set: whom to impact, where to move, for how long, and with what budget.

- *Audience*

Ideally, you should be testing how your campaigns work in different audiences, so as you create them, you will save them from having them ready and filling out this step more quickly. But since this is about setting up a Facebook Ads campaign from scratch, we will stop at each of the steps to take.

You also have the option of using your audiences (called custom audiences) based, for example, on the traffic to your website that the pixel has been able to collect or on contact lists that you can upload yourself.

That is not mandatory because you can also make segmentations based on Facebook's data: location, age, gender, language (in which they have their account configured), and interests and behaviors.

The interests and behaviors are related to characteristics that users have manifested in their profile and consumption of the social network: their profession, their marital status, pages they like. In the case of a cooking blog, we will have more possibilities of generating interest to users interested in this discipline to select related interests: cooking shows, famous chefs, other cooking blogs, brands.

Finally, you can also choose other types of connections related to your page, your app, or your pixel's events. It is especially useful for excluding users you don't want to impact. For example, if what we are looking for is to attract new users to our blog, it would be interesting to avoid those who have already visited us.

As we fill in these options, Facebook will tell us what potential users we can impact with this segmentation and if our segmentation is too specific or too broad:

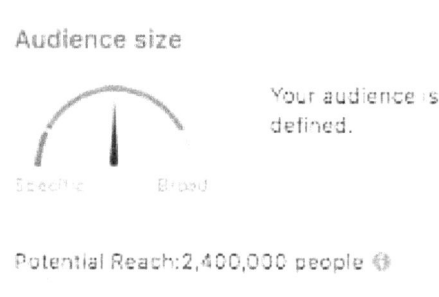

- ***Provision***

The possibilities of placements that Facebook offers is vast and goes beyond the different formats that it can provide within the social network itself, involving other platforms such as Instagram or websites and pages within its network (Audience Network).

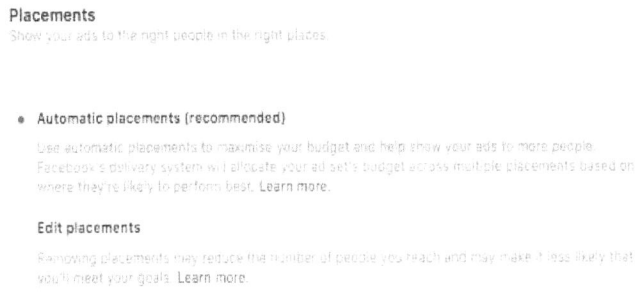

If what we want is to appear in some specific contact points, we must select ourselves from the "Edit Locations" option:

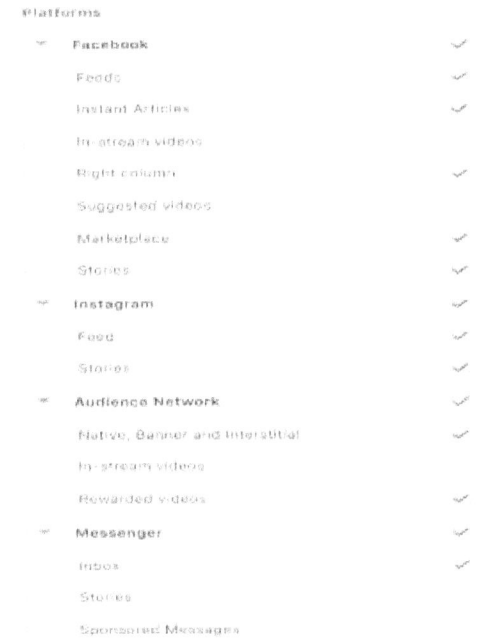

We can also choose which devices to appear on so that if we assume an application developed only for Android. We could avoid leaving on IO devices. If our audience is mostly mobile, eliminate the option to also appear on the desk to optimize investment.

- **Budget and delivery**

It is time to decide how much to invest and when we want to appear.

Regarding the budget, we can choose between defining a total amount for the entire duration of the campaign (I want to consume € 50 that is distributed throughout the whole campaign as Facebook believes optimal), or a daily amount (of the 15 days that my campaign will last, I want 5 € to be consumed every day). It will depend on how uneven or constant you want your investment to be distributed, depending on your pursuits.

You can then decide whether to limit your bid to a specific time or not. Also, a little later, you have the option to choose at what particular times you want your ad to appear and on what days. If your content plays with the context of the time, it will be essential. Imagine that your case consists of promoting an alcohol brand associated with nightlife. Perhaps it makes more sense that your ads appear on weekends from the afternoon tonight than on Monday at 8 in the morning (or not ... it is essential that you try).

And it is time to decide your bid. Again, Facebook lets us choose, this time between automatic bid based on the lowest possible price or maximum bid. Here the recommendation is that if it is the first time you are working with a specific audience and therefore do not know the market costs, choose the first option, and as you get to know the average prices.

Ads

The last piece of the campaign: the ad itself, or what is the same, the format, graphic resource, and message with which you will impact the segment on which you want to achieve a goal.

In the beginning, we talked about the fact decisions made in each of the steps affect the following, so depending on the objective and the location you have chosen, your customization possibilities will be one or the other. If, for example, your idea is to set up an Instagram Stories campaign with targeted traffic, Facebook will give you the option to upload 9:16 videos, but if what you wanted was to bring traffic from Facebook to your website, the options will be different.

Facebook also gives you the option to promote as an ad a post that you have already uploaded organically. In that case, you just have to choose it, and that's it. A tip: if you can't find the publication, you can locate it by entering its ID.

As this is about setting up Facebook Ads campaigns from scratch, we will continue to assume that you do not want to promote something on your wall, but rather that you want to make a publication in parallel. It is known as a dark post (because it is a post that is not seen on your page).

The first thing you will find is the format editor. As you mount campaigns, you will check the effectiveness of each one for your business.

If you have chosen the traffic objective, you will have different text spaces to customize, and again it is best that you go testing the effectiveness of different combinations.

Finally, you can customize the call to action that you want to appear in your ad, depending on your objective: see more, buy, more info ...

As you fill in all the elements, you can see your ad's final result on the right. Check well how it looks in each of the arrangements you have chosen because if, for example, you have selected a headline that is too long, in the desk preview of the ad, it may not be cut, but in the mobile, it does, and that could affect your results.

If you have followed all the steps, you should already have your campaign ready to publish by clicking on the green button that you will see at the editor's bottom right. If there are any errors in what you have configured, do not worry, Facebook usually detects them and warns you through icons with exclamations indicating what the error is.

Chapter 6

LinkedIn Marketing

Still not marketing on LinkedIn? If you only limit yourself to following and accepting contacts, you are wasting the number 1 professional social network and tool that has been on the market since 2003.

LinkedIn has a difference with the rest, and that is that it is a platform focused on the labor and professional world, whose main objective is to connect professionals and companies from all over the world.

Users have a presence on LinkedIn with two objectives:

- ☐ They have a personal profile and want to find a job or promote their brand
- ☐ They seek to promote and increase the visibility of your company

Whether you are on LinkedIn for the first or second reason, you will have to apply a marketing strategy to achieve your goals. And that's what we're going to tell you now, so take note.

How To Use Linkedin For Your Business Or Success

We will go step by step but without forgetting any of the essential factors within this partner platform.

Step #1: Create a Page on Linkedin

Before your company can start using LinkedIn marketing, it needs a LinkedIn page. Here we leave you a quick guide to configure it. If you have not yet created a LinkedIn profile, you will have to do that first.

How to create a LinkedIn Page?

☐ Visit the Linkedin Pages section of the LinkedIn Marketing Solutions website. Click Create a Page.

Fuente: LinkedIn

☐ Choose the correct category for your business.

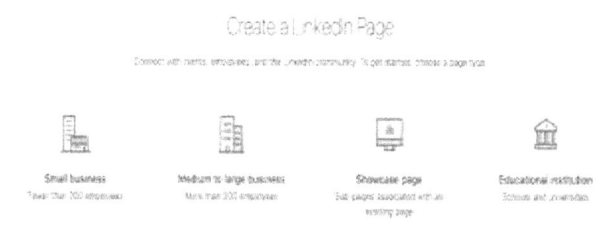

Fuente: LinkedIn

☐ Enter your company details. A preview of the page shows you what it looks like as you add content. Choose the right URL for your brand and, if you can, use the same username that you use on your other social networks.

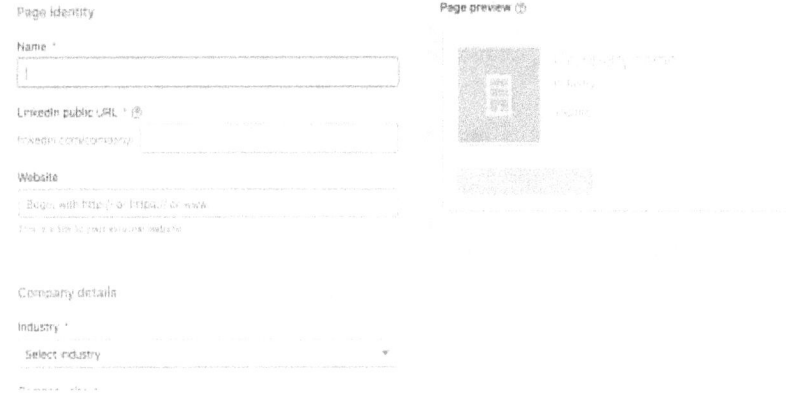

- Upload your company logo and add your slogan. This step is optional, but don't skip it. Companies with logos get six times more visits than those without.

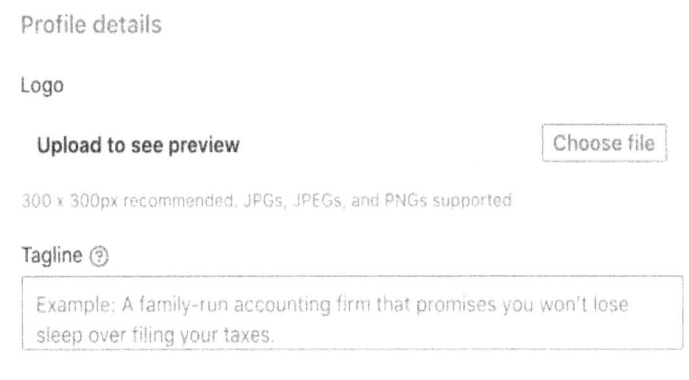

- Click Create Page

Step #2: Complete your Page

Take your LinkedIn Page to the next level by adding more details. That provides visitors with information about your business and improves your ranking in Google and LinkedIn search results. There's a reason full pages get 30% more views.

To add more details, click on the pencil icon below your company name.

Company Description: Tell people about your vision, mission, values, and offer a description of your products and services in 3-4 short paragraphs. The copy must be natural and be written in the voice of your brand. Google results preview up to 156 characters of text on your page, so make your description SEO friendly by including keywords.

Location: Add the location of your store or office. You can add multiple locations by selecting + Add location.

Hashtags: You can add up to 3 hashtags to make your profile easier to search. Pick the hashtags that are popular in your industry and best suited to your business.

Cover Photo: Add some sparkle to your profile with a cover photo. Pick an image that shows what your business is about and avoid shots with too many elements or is cluttered. The recommended size is 1584 (width) x 396 (height) pixels.

Custom button: Add a button to your profile to encourage actions. Options include: visit the website, contact us, get more information, and register. Make sure to add the appropriate URL to click the button land on the correct page. Also, don't forget to add a UTM parameter for tracking.

Manage the language: If you have a global brand or multilingual audience, you can add your name, tagline, and description in more than 20 different languages.

Step #3: Share your page

Let people know that your LinkedIn Page is ready. If you have employees, email the entire company with the news and explain how they can follow the page and add it as a workplace.

Share what makes you proud of the people who make your business a great place. Connect visitors to your company's opinion leaders and give potential customers and employees a glimpse of your work culture.

Also, promote your page with your customers. Use all your digital touchpoints (newsletter, social media, website) and ask them to follow you. When you do, tell people what they can gain from following you, from job opportunities to LinkedIn Live sessions.

On LinkedIn, Page administrators can also invite their contacts to follow them. Just click on the Admin Tools drop-down menu in the top right corner and select Invite Members.

Step #4: Add LinkedIn buttons

Add social media icons to the header or footer of your website or newsletter so that people can find your LinkedIn page easier. Find the most up-to-date version of the LinkedIn logo and branding guidelines here. Also, you can save the following images.

You can also add Share and Follow buttons with LinkedIn Plugins.

Step #5: Create a LinkedIn Marketing Strategy

Once you have your company page ready, it is time to start thinking about your marketing strategy for LinkedIn.

What goals can your company achieve on LinkedIn? Are you going to use LinkedIn to hire people, for social sales, connect with your customers, or all of the above? Should Your LinkedIn Marketing Budget Include Ads?

Know the demographics of LinkedIn. It is a good starting point for knowing who is using the platform and whom you can reach. Conduct an audit of your competitors on LinkedIn. See how they use the forum, what works, and how you can make your page stand out.

Create a content calendar for LinkedIn. This way, you can plan your content ahead of time, get images, write thought leadership articles, and prepare your content accordingly. That also allows you to make sure that all of your LinkedIn marketing goals are covered, from promoting webinars to engaging.

Visual tools like Hootsuite Planner provide a clear picture of your content plan, making it easier for you to spot things that are not working well and allowing you to strike the right balance.

Advertising Opportunities

You already know how to create your business page on LinkedIn. Now is the time to move on to marketing your business. Are you looking for the best marketing tips and tricks on LinkedIn to help you optimize your B2B business and B2B lead generation efforts?

This section tells you how to develop the best LinkedIn marketing tactics to help your business grow.

7 Powerful LinkedIn Marketing Tips That Will Grow Your Business

Tip #1. Identify your goals

As with any marketing initiative, it is crucial to identify your goals.

Common B2B marketing goals for LinkedIn can include:

- Increase your brand profile and authority
- Generate, nurture and capture leads
- Drive relevant traffic to your website
- Promote appearances at events

Once you clearly define your goals, it's easier to formulate a marketing plan that works.

Tip #2. Complete your company profile

That is one of the essential LinkedIn marketing tips since your company profile is your brand's soul online.

It is imperative to have a solid profile to show people looking for your business online and who want to know about your products and services.

Your business profile is where most of the people in your target market go when they first click on your page, and you only get one chance to make an excellent first impression.

These are some tips to complete an excellent company profile:

- Make sure you complete 100% of your profile without leaving any spaces.
- It almost goes without saying, but avoid typos and grammar mistakes.
- See your competitors' profile and think about what you can do to make your business stand out.

- ☐ If you have recently received awards or honors related to your industry, write them down on a list.

- ☐ If you have any known clients, ask for their permission and mention them on your profile.

- ☐ Always include a link to your business website. If people like what they read on your profile, they will want to know more.

- ☐ Make sure to use the banner space it provides you wisely. Think of the banner as the front of your online store. Make it work for you.

Completing the LinkedIn profile is vital.

It allows your company to be found in searches and will enable you to surprise your potential customers.

Plus, it gives you the credibility you need to convince potential customers to contact you on LinkedIn and start a conversation.

Tip #3. Optimize your search page for LinkedIn marketing

An excellent company profile is useless if people have a hard time finding it. To help you use Search Engine Optimization (SEO), read the [top eight SEO trends for 2020.](#)

Insert your company's keywords in your profile. Choose relevant keywords that clearly describe your business and what you offer.

Not sure which keywords to use?

Start by asking yourself what keywords or phrases a prospect would type into Google to search for your product or service.

Tip #4. Share content for marketing on LinkedIn

Once you've set up your profile, it's time to start creating content.

Content marketing is crucial for any social media platform, and LinkedIn is no exception.

Content marketing on LinkedIn can be more successful than on any other channel.

On LinkedIn, you have a captive audience of professionals eager for knowledge and information.

There are 91% of executives rate LinkedIn as their first choice for professionally relevant content.

Share blogs, webinars, and videos based on topics relevant to your target market.

One of the essential marketing tips is to focus on quality.

If possible, reach out to your industry opinion leaders who are active on LinkedIn and ask for their input.

Sharing content periodically helps you create an audience that returns to your page every week.

Use free tools

Content marketing doesn't require a big budget. There are many free tools that you can use to create graphics and videos:

- [Canva](#) - A free graphic design tool
- [Unsplash](#) - A library of free high-resolution images
- [Piktochart](#) - An infographic creator
- [Lumen5](#): convert text to video in minutes

Here are some of the best practices for sharing content:

- High-value posts (new content or high-engagement events) work best Tuesday through Thursday.

- Low-value posts (re-shares, repurposing, old content), Monday or Friday

- Post headers must be 40-69 characters long (including spaces). If it is more than 220 characters, the copy is broken, and the rest is hidden.

- The best performing headline types include questions, lists, and how-to guides.

- Use hashtags carefully and on a new line when possible.

- The links are usually a piece/page to pull the image and increase the click area. Use a tracking link when possible.

- Occasionally write an attractive copy from a personal account and link in the comments.

Tip #5. Grow your network for LinkedIn marketing

One of the marketing tips on LinkedIn to gain new followers is to do a combination of these five methods:

- Make sure all your employees follow your company page and like posts. They are the most prominent advocates for the brand and the most likely to share your content.

- Invite your customers and partners to follow your page. Promote your presence on LinkedIn on their blogs, email newsletters, and press releases.

- Share other people's content, especially if it's relevant or posted by an influencer in your industry.

- Tag the connections in your content promotions if you think it will be useful.

- Ask your successful clients to write testimonials and recommendations for your company page.

Tip #6. Don't be afraid to experiment

When you've mastered the basics of LinkedIn marketing, it's time to branch out.

Experiment with posts at different times of the day or week. If a particular type of post gets more engagement than others, make more similar ones. Analyze the pages of your competition.

How effectively do they use LinkedIn? Do they do something that you do too? Or, on the contrary, is there something they are not doing that you can do?

Look for the gaps that exist in your sector and try to fill them.

Tip #7. Always measure your marketing results on LinkedIn

To improve data-driven marketing on LinkedIn, review your efforts regularly.

It includes a standard reporting feature, or if you don't use one, LinkedIn's analytics pages provide a wealth of information.

LinkedIn Analytics is divided into three sections:

- *Visitor analysis*

It gives you all the information you need to know about the people who click on your page, including:

> The total number of page views and unique visitors over time

> The proportion of visitors from desktop computers and mobile devices

> Demographic information, such as your role at work, location, industry, and company size

☐ *Analysis update*

Engagement metrics for all your LinkedIn posts include:

> The total number of likes, comments, clicks, and shares you've had during a specified time

> The interaction relationship between organic and sponsored content (if you are running any ads on LinkedIn)

> Post-by-post real-time data, including impressions, views, clicks, and aggregate LinkedIn engagement rate

☐ *Followers analysis*

It offers you all the information you need about your audience, including:

> The total number of followers and new followers for the last 30 days

> Demographics of all your followers (where they live and work)

> A competitor's tracker, which compares your followers and updates with those of other similar companies

Marketing on LinkedIn undoubtedly helps your business develop. When it comes to professional online networking, it is at the forefront of most people's minds.

Your business must have a presence that stands out, and you must make the most of the opportunities it offers you.

These LinkedIn marketing strategies will help you design a social media marketing plan for your business. Put them into practice and track your progress.

Chapter 7

Instagram Marketing

It appeared in 2010 as any other social network, more like a photo gallery without, at least for the first time, another objective than to upload photos.

Taking a step forward and planting ourselves today, digital marketing is not understood without Instagram's presence.

Right now, Instagram is a mobile application. However, it also has the Instagram web option (although with fewer opportunities for use than the app), allowing you to upload images, videos with effects and filters, etc. which has many different purposes: increasing the visibility of companies and advertising.

How To Market On Instagram

We will see the best marketing strategies on Instagram that can help you sell as a personal brand or your eCommerce with your products.

Each of these points is very important, so you should try to carry them all out as much as possible.

#1. Optimize your bio

This point is essential when you create your Instagram account since if someone finds us on the social network, they should see what we do and what we do without taking too many detours.

Therefore, watch [this video](#) that shows you through a real example to optimize your Instagram profile.

#2. Include the link to your portfolio

Continuing with the previous example, it is essential that you include the website of your project in your profile bio (nothing new that you do not know, right?), So if what you want to promote is a part of your website as a portfolio of courses includes that URL.

Many people enter a link in this section, a connection that opens different links so that you have more than one option to visit, not just the link to your main website.

#3. Use the stories

Using Instagram stories to generate marketing is about only going out to eat and uploading a photo of what you are doing, but it goes much further.

If you have an eCommerce or a company, it is best to upload stories about your products, and above all, a tip would be that you and your team go out presenting the work. Humanizing the brand is the best thing you can do to make your audience connect more.

If you want to enhance your brand and are clear about what you want to do, you should make stories telling your day-to-day work, giving tips and advice, and teaching other interesting topics related to your sector so that they still identify you more with what you do.

#4. Make use of questions and answers

It is essential that you interact with the followers in your stories, and what better way than asking them about your products, their personal preferences, tastes, or any questions you have.

You must make your followers participate at all times and make them feel close to you. You have to make them feel part of your brand and know that you are listening to them.

Many influencers use this technique, and with this, they manage to connect with their audience. They will also win retractors, yes, but too many people who admire them.

Another technique is that the followers themselves ask you, and you respond with the stories; you will make them feel more identified with the people behind them.

#5. Use featured stories

The highlights or highlighted stories are the icons that we see under the bio, and they are the stories that we have previously uploaded but that we want to highlight in our profile for a specific reason.

We can divide them according to the themes that we will cover: Design, events, food, questions, shopping.

You must create some great stories and upload them to your Instagram profile with designs according to your brand or company.

#6. Post regularly with planned content

Neither go overboard nor fall short. That's the key.

But right now, you will be asking yourself: Bego, how many times do I publish a week?

The answer is… IT DEPENDS. When is your target audience connected? How do you generate more engagement?

The key in marketing to know the frequency of publication on Instagram is experimentation: test, test, and keep testing.

It is said that the Instagram algorithm favors accounts that have posts regularly, so it is time for you to start with it and increase the interactions of your account.

Also, all this content must be previously planned in an editorial calendar so that there is no day that we run out of ideas.

#7. Use Hashtags

Using hashtags is an essential strategy to achieve a greater reach in our publications.

My advice is to include smaller and more specific hashtags, as they will be more sought after by the target audience, so there is a greater chance that someone who reaches them will keep our Instagram account and want to continue browsing through it.

However, if we use generic hashtags, it can cover many areas, and we will not be focusing on the target that we want to send our publications.

But beware, excessive use of hashtags or incorrect use can damage your reach and be affected by the Instagram shadowban. Use them wisely.

#8. Network and interact

If you have ever read my newsletter, you will know that Networking is essential since you know people with whom you can create incredible synergies, and social networks are a way to make them.

We must generate relationships through Instagram as a marketing strategy and also interact in their publications so that the Instagram algorithm sees us with good eyes.

#9. Create a company profile

Do you know the advantages of having a company profile on Instagram? If not, I will name them in a very straightforward way so that you can start creating yours right now:

- ☐ You have statistics about your audience's connection time, countries, cities, age, and gender.
- ☐ You can include in your BIO a button to contact, call or know where you are

- It provides you with the number of visits to your profile, clicks on your website, emails that have been sent to you through the social network

- It gives you statistics on your posts and stories

#10. Monitor your followers

You already know what is said in marketing (and with good reason). You will never win if you don't measure.

We must monitor both our brand and our followers on Instagram, and what better way than seeing the type of profile they are (with company statistics) and knowing other data that we will extract from results analysis tools. Ideally, plan all of this in an Instagram audit.

On the other hand, we also have external applications that tell us whom the account's best followers are based on their interactions, so the right way is to reward them for their loyalty.

#11. Create an attractive feed for your audience

I love this part since we must create an attractive feed according to our target audience.

We must see if we will create a puzzle profile with graphic design or a feed with very well edited photographs.

Once you've decided, it's time to get into the action with photo editing, and here your creativity comes into play and what you've learned from both free and paid design programs.

#12. Use Instagram advertising

Organic reach is significant, yes, but we can also reach many more people with an advertising-based strategy, right?

And why don't we use it?

To start doing marketing and advertising campaigns on Instagram effectively, we must be clear about a series of aspects:

- Who is the target audience of the brand and the campaigns?
- We want to advertise (stories, timeline) and what type of advertisement (video, carousel, image).
- What budget are we going to invest in?

Once these aspects are apparent, we will create our Facebook Ads account, install the Facebook pixel, and carry out the campaigns.

#13. Use techniques to improve engagement

Have striking photos and images, create copies (texts) that attract attention and encourage comments, or make videos that people cannot resist leaving their opinion.

We must perform these actions to increase the engagement of our publications and our account.

And if you are still unsure how to obtain your Instagram account's engagement, here is a compilation of how to extract it using formulas depending on publication type.

#14. Make live videos

Video marketing is present in any Instagram and marketing strategy since these publications tend to generate greater engagement due to hook users' ability.

Conducting live interviews with other accounts is a widespread technique in the digital marketing sector and live videos for the vast majority of industries, or videos humanizing brands.

It is essential that we plan this strategy to carry it out correctly and thus impact our followers with well-edited and well-worked videos.

#15. Use Instagram shopping if you are an eCommerce

When Instagram shopping came to light, it was like a revolution of the social network since we saw products tagged in the brand's publications, and could even mean the end of other social networks such as 21Buttons.

If you have an eCommerce, it is time you start using this technique, as it can lead to a reasonably large increase in your company's sales.

#16. Take into account the Instagram algorithm

The Instagram algorithm is always changing and adding different functions, so what I'm going to tell you today may no longer be worth tomorrow.

It is said that when you post a photo or video on Instagram, the algorithm shows it to around 10% of your followers. If this 10% interacts with your publication, the algorithm will consider its quality content and increase its reach.

On the contrary, if this 10% do not interact with the content, they probably will not show it to many more people.

Therefore, we must make this 10% interact and get them to like and comment as soon as possible to reach a greater reach. Are you willing to try it?

#17. Analyze your results

measure, and you will win.

To see if what we are doing is working and performing well, we must analyze through statistics to know the interests of the audience we are targeting, which publications are using, and when to publish.

For this, I recommend you 5 Tools To Decode Your Target Audience.

A Brief Comparison To Snapchat

The war between Instagram and Snapchat is more intense than ever. And is that, since Instagram implemented Instagram Stories, the growth of Snapchat has seen its development jeopardized. But what do these two competing platforms have in common? Will Snapchat be able to trace its success? Most importantly, how can you take advantage of these tools' potential in your company?

Not only Twitter has competitors, but Snapchat too. Although Instagram already existed before the birth of Snapchat in 2011, it has begun to be a threat to the app created by and for millennials since it integrated Instagram Stories, whose concept is very similar to how Snapchat works.

There is no doubt that some functionalities of Snapchat have inspired Instagram, and this has done much damage to a tool that promised to be very interesting for users and brands. These are the ideas that Instagram has borrowed from the messaging network:

- **Instagram Stories**

Observing the success of Snapchat stories, Instagram launched Instagram Stories, which works the same as Snapchat: images and videos that can be viewed on users' profiles for 24 hours.

- **Accessories**

Also following in the wake of Snapchat, Instagram gave its users the ability to include text and emojis in their stories. Also, it is allowed to sketch drawings in publications with three different types of pointers.

- **Filters**

Instagram's next action was to integrate animated filters for their stories' photos and videos, the main point of differentiation that Snapchat had. This resource is beautiful, especially for younger users.

- **Location**

Finally, the social network bought by Facebook has announced a new feature for Instagram Stories: the ability to find stories by location or by hashtag.

The future of Snapchat

After the unstoppable advance of Instagram, many wonders if Snapchat will survive. Although we will only know the definitive answer in time, the truth is that the data poses a bleak future for Snapchat. In its short life, Instagram Stories already has 200 million daily active users, thus surpassing the 160 million Snapchat. Snapchat can only try to reinvent itself and provide new services that differentiate it from Instagram.

Snapchat vs. Instagram

1-Users registered on Snapchat and Instagram

Instagram is ideal for promotions and advertising since it has many registered users (summarized in a greater reach with less effort).

You can do the test: ask your friends if they have this social network, and you will be surprised to see that almost all your friends have an Instagram account, but a low percentage of them have a Snapchat account.

2-Interface and functionalities

Snapchat is an exclusive tool for sharing photos and videos live with our circle of friends. It allows you to create groups of chats between friends, as well as send private messages.

On the other hand, Instagram is a tool where you can share even more since we can make publications (photos, videos, GIFs) in our feed, and there is also a stories section that is where we can share photos and videos live. Also, Instagram has an available area called IG TV, where we can see longer videos.

How Instagram Is Like Twitter With Picture

Twitter is a relatively long-lived social network compared to Instagram since it was released to the public in mid-2006, gaining reliable recognition and fame since then.

Instagram, for its part, was inaugurated in 2010, acquiring rapid popularity among young audiences.

Both networks have different directions and configurations. However, despite their differences, many people cannot avoid establishing a relationship and subsequent comparison between both systems, ensuring that one is better than the other or that its functionalities are complete and extensive.

For its part, Twitter is a microblogging social network based on rapid communication through a message published on the user's home page. This message is called "Tweet" and whose length does not exceed 280 characters.

It is a network where long messages are not allowed, which has made it recognized among some communities as "the Internet SMS."

In another sense, Instagram is a social network and a mobile application for smartphones based on sharing photos under your user profile, which you can modify and apply certain textures using specific tools provided by the application.

It is an app that became quite popular after its launch due to the novelty of the interface and how practical it is to share photos taken with the smartphone camera almost instantly.

These networks have several differences, which stand out significantly when looking closely at both platforms.

Twitter is primarily intended for desktop applications for computers, so it is accessed through its web address.

Instead, Instagram was designed for smartphones and tablets to access it through an application acquired through the App Store.

Studies according to Number of Users and Time of Use

A study showed by ComScore, in which certain aspects are taken as crucial points for the evaluation, such as:

- Users over 18 years of age
- Official mobile application users
- Participation takes into account only the average time per unique user.

In this study, it was found that there is a more significant number of users on Instagram at the moment and that they spend 257 minutes in the Instagram application sharing, ranking, and commenting on photos.

That is a relatively high average usage compared to the 170 minutes in which Twitter users remain immersed on the web reading Tweets.

Chapter 8

YouTube Marketing

Indeed you have read previously in the Google algorithm chapters regarding SEO positioning techniques and strategies, right? Well, each social network has its algorithm, and YouTube could not be less.

The first thing to keep in mind is that more than 400 hours of content are uploaded per minute, which means that competition is very high. Therefore, your videos' quality must be excellent if you want to stand out and create a loyal and faithful community.

No matter what type of content you upload to your YouTube channel, you will only have to worry about defining and following a good strategy on YouTube.

Defining a strategy, as well as measuring its results, are critical requirements for any marketing action.

It is convenient to know what YouTube values for the positioning of the videos. Keep in mind that the most significant interest of this social network is to get the greatest number of people to interact with it for as long as possible and therefore, the videos that have the longest playing time and the most visited ones will be the ones that position the best, all this roughly. So, now the question is the following:

How To Market On YouTube?

When we face a YouTube marketing strategy, there are specific parameters that remain in the pipeline. We will try to approach them from the most basic to not create a complex of reading and not taking action, procrastinating again and again.

1-Planning your YouTube strategy

TO PLAN. Plan as much as you can (and a little more) your YouTube strategy. The more long-term you think, the better, because your content's quality will be better and it will be more work.

Here are some tips to follow in your YouTube strategy:

- Calculate the time it can take to record and edit a video to know how often you can upload one to your channel.

- Create a posting calendar. This way, you will have time to script all your videos and save time in the recording.

- Answer one of the most critical questions: What do I want to position? When you have a clear answer, you can select the keywords or keywords and work on them more thoroughly to better your channel's positioning.

- Work on branding, both brand (if it is what you are selling) and yours. Having the public identify you as an expert in your sector is incredibly useful for positioning.

- By planning your YouTube strategy, you can identify and, therefore, anticipate creating quality content. Keep in mind that selling from YouTube is not an easy task. On the other hand, generating interest is.

- Therefore, content planning and defining your YouTube strategy is key to being successful.

There are three essential points that we have to take into account when making a YouTube Marketing strategy, and they are the following:

2-Quality Content

Tell a story close to you and not try to be something unreal or create a TV ad for YouTube. That strategy does not work here. What works is the closeness, trust, and transparency of your business, whether sole proprietorship or company. And to create this type of material, you have to be very close to your clients or external users, knowing what they are demanding of you, these videos being the answer to their needs, not yours.

Here your strategy must be based on Inbound Marketing and not on the old Outbound Marketing and let me explain a bit:

- Attraction marketing is when your content ends up from its good positioning in search engines (SEO).
- Good content movement strategy on Social Networks (SMM)
- The correct conversion of the visit into a customer
- The ability to analyze content to know if it is working or not
- Above all, listen and improve with that active listening. And how? Well, through the same comments on your channel, the feedback you can receive through Social Networks, with your closest circle of friends and family

3-SEO for YouTube

Very important to be positioned in those words in which we believe our users can be, and for this, we must do internal or external work to know what these are. And on these, start generating content around you to be found without resorting to the old strategies. We can use the AdWords keyword tool. Or YouTube.

And for this, I remind you of the conditions that will make our content gain presence on YouTube:

- Title First the Keywords and then the branding

- Description (5000 characters) Take advantage of the first 250, which are the ones you see without having to click on "Show more"

- Tags NO Spam. The most important keywords at the beginning.

- Add them to Playlist. Gather the videos into lists like p. ex. "Product reviews."

- The age of the video

- The times it has been shared on Social Networks

- Entry links and times it has been embedded in other sites.

- Number of comments

- Number of Likes

- The Annotations. Don't forget to create a series of annotations that will make the user spend more time on your channel.

- The video contains as a name our main keyword (videobranding.mp4) and not (00098.mp4)

- YouTube likes the .mp4 format with the H264 codec to export in our editor and later upload. And at 720p.

4-Audience and Engagement

In this part, we will address how to be proactive in the YouTube account.

- There are a series of parameters to enable in the account, allowing users to comment without the need for approval located in "Default values," including the video response. And you have to be quick when responding because that speed will make you better connect with your audience.

☐ Connect account with "Influencers" of your sector. Keep up to date with the movements and enter to comment on their content. If you have communication with them, others interested in your niche will be able to reach you, that if very delicately, no Spam, providing valuable content and comments.

☐ Use the promotion services of Google AdWords for video, well-optimized the campaign, and with a good ad can be very profitable. Remember that you only paid per click on your ad and asked the other day an AdWords consultant, more specifically Sergio Falcón (@runical). The CTR ranges between 4-7 cents per click.

☐ It is evident, but at the same time, you upload the video, post it on your blog, and promote it on RRSS.

Tools For YouTube

If you want to reach a growing audience that your videos are seen and liked, you better take a look at one of these tools. Who knows how many followers you can get by changing a couple of things on your channel?

1-YouTube Analytics

YouTube Analytics is the YouTube version of Google Analytics, Google's visitor measurement tool.

Like its counterpart for web pages, YouTube Analytics will allow you to analyze the visits to your channel, the views of your videos, the demographic profile of your visitors, if they watch the entire videos or lose their attention at some point, from where your visits (do they look for you on YouTube? do they access you from social networks?), comments, likes and dislikes.

You will be able to limit by periods and generate reports to analyze calmly and improve your strategy as YouTubers.

2-Keyword Tool for YouTube

Keyword Tool is an efficient tool for YouTubers to answer that question. You can narrow down by language and country and, from a word, get related topics to sharpen your aim when tagging YouTube videos.

In addition to keywords, you are offered frequently asked questions from those searching for something on YouTube, which is very useful for video tutorials. For example, if we search for Photoshop, we get How to download Photoshop, use Photoshop, draw in Photoshop, blur ...

With the Keyword Tool, you can also search for keywords on Google, Bing, Amazon, and the Apple App Store.

3-VidIQ

If YouTube Analytics falls short and you need to know in detail what your audience is like and how to grow it, one option is VidIQ.

VidIQ allows you to know the impact of your videos inside and outside the portal. That is, also, on social networks. You will get tips to improve your videos' tagging so you can appear more often in related videos.

You can also monitor your competitors and thus get closer to them in visits and followers.

4-YouTube Trends

Returning to YouTube and its tools for YouTubers, you will find topics that have had or are relevant in YouTube searches in YouTube Trends.

Either for seasonal reasons or viral reasons, YouTube Trends allows you to dive by categories and know the trends that are growing the most.

It is updated little once a month, but it allows you to analyze events that have been very successful, examples of videos that have taken advantage of that event, and anticipate next year.

5-Social Blade

If you want to meet the greats of YouTube, in Social Blade, you will find a powerful ally that will allow you to see the lists of the most successful YouTubers, what type of content they produce, how many followers they have.

Social Blade offers daily and monthly statistics, as well as estimated earnings. In addition to making you envious, the information on this analysis page will allow you to see similar channels, which videos have worked best, and thus make changes and improvements to your own YouTube channel.

Another efficient function is to compare up to three different channels. It will allow you to know who is doing the best and what you need to do to get closer to the most critical YouTubers.

6-TubeBuddy

It is one of the complete tools for YouTubers that you will find.

TubeBuddy is installed in Google Chrome through an extension and integrates with YouTube adding dozens of new functions that will help you better manage the upload and personalization of videos, the configuration of your channel, the measurement of audiences.

By default, it is free, although to use all its functions, you need one of the different paid versions, depending on the number of followers you have and the level of professionalism you want to achieve.

TubeBuddy will also help you to better tag your videos, to promote them on social networks, to analyze the data generated

Chapter 9

Marketing on Pinterest

We have previously seen that social media's digital ecosystem seems to be dominated by brands such as Facebook, Instagram, YouTube, and Twitter, as these are the social networks with the largest number of active users in the world.

However, when carrying out digital marketing campaigns, many companies and agencies focus their attention (and their investment) on a smaller social network, but with enormous strategic potential: Pinterest, which already has more than 300 million users.

Ecommerce Stores And Retailers Data

To better understand the business impact that Pinterest has for companies in the social media ecosystem, let's look at the following ten facts about this platform in business:

1. 80% of millennials say that Pinterest helps them find products they want to buy, while 71% use the platform to find recommendations on what to buy.

2. In general, millennials prefer to use Pinterest to make purchases over any other social network. Almost 50% of them have bought a product with which they have interacted within the platform.

3. 87% of pinners (Pinterest users) have bought articles that they have seen on this platform, and 93% of them plan to do so.

4. 90% of weekly users use Pinterest to make purchase decisions, whether they end up making them simultaneously or later, online or offline. Even 72% do it to decide what to buy offline.

5. 55% of pinners use the platform incredibly to search for products, a behavior that is four times higher compared to other social networks.

6. Proportionally based on the number of users, Pinterest generates 33% more shopping traffic than Facebook, 71% more than Snapchat, and 200% more than Twitter.

7. 77% of users have discovered a new brand or product within the platform.

8. 78% of users say that brands' content is useful, while more than 75% of pins pinned (saved publications) come from brands, companies, and businesses.

9. Digital campaigns on Pinterest generate almost four times more sales compared to those on other platforms.

10. 96% of active pinners use Pinterest to research and plan events like weddings or trips, for example.

Although the top is dominated by Google's ecosystems (YouTube) and Facebook (Facebook, Facebook Messenger, Instagram, and WhatsApp), Pinterest has characteristics that make it the most powerful digital marketing platform in certain specific contexts.

Six strategies to use Pinterest in your business effectively

Once we have covered many critical aspects of Pinterest in some depth, you are ready to learn six practical strategies that you must implement in your Pinterest marketing strategy to obtain excellent results:

Strategy #1: Determine the best time to post your pins

As you already know, a great advantage is that the pins can last forever. However, if you build a community that is usually connected to Pinterest at certain times, it will be essential to consider when choosing at what time of the day to update your profile.

An essential tool to know this type of information is Pinterest Analytics.

You can also consult studies and reports that address this issue of days and hours, although you should know that, in general, each study gives different results. That is because the data varies depending on each business's nature, the audiences, and the markets.

For example,

- According to each category, the best days to post are:
  - Monday: fitness
  - Tuesday: gadgets and technology
  - Wednesday: thematic or inspirational phrases
  - Thursday: outfits
  - Friday: gifts
  - Saturday: travel
  - Sunday: food, art, and leisure
- Some of the best times to post are:
  - Between 2 a.m. and 4 a.m
  - Between 8 p.m. and 11 p.m. (or 1 a.m.)
  - Between 2 p.m. and 4 p.m

As we have seen, these data can be the first reference to take into account, but they are very subjective. As time passes, you need to begin to be guided by your own Pinterest Analytics data.

One particular thing is that we do not recommend publishing during business hours, since at those times, the active audience of Pinterest is tiny (according to each niche).

Strategy #2: Post on trending topics and use calls to action on your pin

By using CTAs on your images, you can increase engagement levels by 80%, while if you post on trending topics, your CTR can increase up to 94%.

To find out about trends on Pinterest, you can use two potent tools that Pinterest launched in 2019:

> ➤ One of them is Pinterest Trends, which provides you with insights on the most popular search terms in the last twelve months.

> ➤ The other is Pinterest 100, an interactive report on the top 100 search trends in 10 specific subject categories.

Strategy #3: Enable the pins button

Make sure you have the pins button enabled on your website. In this way, users will save the images from the web to their personal Pinterest account, even when they are offline. This way, you will be able to feedback on the visits to your page since the user will surely return to consult that pin that he saved.

Strategy #4: Add a link to your pins

Generating traffic to your website is one of the pillars of Pinterest marketing strategies. Always link each of the pins to your website or your products (in the case of eCommerce). And you can do this only by placing the link on the respective pin.

Strategy #5: Be consistent in your posts

Pinterest rewards consistency (and punishes a lack of it). If you have a company profile and do not keep it active for a specific time, the platform could penalize your pins' positioning, even if you did everything else well.

Strategy #6: Keep in mind Pinterest Ads

Although organic positioning is advantageous, investing in promoting your pins can ensure much faster and more robust growth. Remember that advertising on Pinterest is the cheapest of all social networks.

Best practices on Pinterest

Depending on the type of business and target audience you have, your presence on this social network will make more or less sense. But if you already have it clear, I leave you some acceptable Pinterest practices:

Make your profile striking: as in any social network, you must take care of your profile image. Choose a good photograph or your logo for the avatar and make a complete description. It is also recommended that you change your profile to a company profile.

Create thematic boards: the boards you publish have to be consistent with your brand and be easily identifiable. Take good care of the title, description, and tags.

Focus your activity on your website: on Pinterest, you can link the images you upload to a website, so take advantage of it!

Give it a touch of storytelling: as in any social network, it is best that you generate quality content. And even better if you tell a story with your images.

Don't just talk about your brand: and, starting from the previous point, it is essential that you don't just talk about yourself. It is good that you have a more corporate board, but the best thing is that you upload or share useful and quality content.

Interact with other users: Pinterest is a social network, so the way to gain followers is by interacting with other users and their boards/pins.

How to direct traffic from Pinterest to your website or blog

As said, on Pinterest, you have the possibility of generating traffic to your website and, therefore, leads. It is achieved, in addition to the main link of the profile, thanks to adding a URL in the images.

To do this, when you go to upload a new image, you must enter the destination URL. For example, it is beneficial when you upload an illustration linked to a post on your blog.

Another option that can come in handy if you carry out inbound marketing actions is to share your downloadables' landings. Thus, in addition to getting traffic, it is also very likely that they will later convert to a lead or registration.

What you should keep in mind is not to upload any image to Pinterest to link it to your blog. Try to design a very visual or illustrated embodiment to look like just a container for links.

Chapter 10

Other Marketing Tools To Get Success

Digital Marketing tools are specific examples of solutions that companies have sought to reduce the Cost of Customer Acquisition (CAC). Whether in the implementation of advanced or basic strategies, these are used by many types of businesses.

This chapter will learn about the most critical types of Digital Marketing tools and how they can help you streamline and optimize your company's actions on online channels.

Marketing Automation Tool

Marketing Automation tools involve many functionalities, such as Landing Pages, Email Marketing, and email automation flows. That facilitates and extends the management of leads and their maturity in the sales funnel.

That translates into an increase in the volume of more prepared Leads that will be sent for Sales and improvements in team productivity, as the process can be automated through predetermined triggers.

Email Marketing Tool

Email Marketing is one of the leading customer relationship channels. After the visitor has the first contact with your company and becomes Lead, it is through Email Marketing that you communicate with him and offer him more content until he is ready to speak with the sales team.

1-Mailjet

This tool serves more than 150 countries and seeks to be a global solution for all email marketing needs.

The free plan allows you to have an unlimited number of contacts, a clear advantage over other free email marketing tools. What is limited is the number of emails you can send: 200 a day or 6000 a month. To eliminate this limit and Mailjet branding and have 24/7 support, you can choose one of their payment plans, starting at $ 9.65 per month.

2-[Mailify](#)

Mailify is an email marketing, bulk SMS, and marketing automation tool. It offers an intuitive editor, EmailBuilder, to design beautiful newsletters and responsive templates, and professional HD images for free download. It presents accessible smart functionalities such as Predictive Shipping, Heatmap, Interval Shipping.

With the free version, you can send up to 500 emails. What differentiates it from its competitors is that unlimited contacts can be imported, it is available in 6 languages (French, English, Spanish, Portuguese, German, and Dutch), it can be connected with more than 30 applications (Google Analytics, WordPress, PrestaShop) and offers free consultancies in all languages.

3-[SendPulse](#)

This free email tool is relatively new, but it has gotten much positive feedback from users.

The free plan allows you to send up to 15,000 emails per month to a database of up to 2,500 users. Payment plans, starting at $ 9.85 per month, also allow you to send SMS and push notifications.

Besides being generous with sending limits, this tool also has a straightforward interface, so it is ideal for getting started in email marketing.

If you want to find more tools for your email marketing, click [here](#).

Landing page creation tool

Landing Pages are pages that are intended to receive visitors and convert them into Leads. After that conversion, the visitor becomes a contact or business opportunity.

Through Landing Pages, we offer relevant materials and other currencies that seek to convince the visitor to register their data, such as name, email, telephone number, and company.

In this way, it is possible to establish a relationship with the Lead and send them more content, according to their profile and needs. Click here to find more tools.

Content Marketing Platform

Many companies still do not use platforms to control and document their content planning and production strategies.

These tools can significantly optimize the process because they allow everything from blog management to creating demands for the production of posts, saving time, and increasing efficiency.

Local SEO and Review Marketing

Local SEO (Local Search Engine Optimization), sometimes referred to as local search marketing, is an incredibly effective way to market your local business online as it helps companies promote their products and services to local customers at the exact moment they are searching for them online.

That is accomplished through various methods, some of which differ significantly from what is practiced in standard SEO, and some of which are much easier to manage using local SEO tools and may require marketing services from local search or specific SEO.

Analytics tool

Measuring your online actions results is essential for you to get the best data from your business. You can do it through the use of the Analytics platforms.

Among the advantages of using this type of platform is the evaluation and understanding of the visitors' interest in the site.

In this way, it is possible to measure the return on investment (ROI) of the actions carried out and detect which activities and strategies generate more results to attract and interest the public.

CMS (Content Management System)

Managing the publication of content on sites and blogs is essential to have the help of a Content Management System (CMS).

These tools make it possible to create, edit, and publish all kinds of content and attach content posted on other platforms, such as YouTube videos or podcasts.

Social Media Monitoring Tool

Social network monitoring software helps in the optimization of the actions in the networks. These tools stimulate productivity growth through post scheduling and allow you to track brand mentions, assess interest and reactions to content, and the fan base.

What can be perceived is that the use of Digital Marketing tools is becoming more popular, but there is still much room for companies to improve their processes through these solutions. It is also possible to perceive that business opportunities want to create new technological solutions for Digital Marketing.

Chapter 11

New Ways To Social And Go Marketing

We have seen that we live in a fascinating time for innovative marketing and branding actions, which are actively nourished, especially by new communication tools through Social Networks and the Internet. Everything can be created and fed with the recipients' reactions until a global message with local interest is achieved.

We live in a fascinating time for innovative marketing and branding actions, which are actively nourished, especially by new communication tools through Social Networks and the Internet. Everything can be created and fed with the recipients' reactions until a global message with local interest is achieved.

What To Do

> **Find the right channels**

When you have a target market and reach them effectively, you need to identify the right channel through which to transmit your content. The type of medium you choose will depend on the target audience you have. For example, visual-based marketing strategies may perform well on Pinterest or Instagram, while B2C (consumer business) marketing will perform better on Facebook and Pinterest.

> **Post original content**

Stand out and be known through publications with original and high-quality content aimed at a target audience is a strategy that will be very popular and will be remembered. If you are looking to obtain the best results in your content strategy, make sure to adapt all the content of your website, blog, and social networks to the target audience. That valuable and relevant content will be what will allow your business to position your business on the first page of Google searches. Make sure the content you produce answers questions, solves problems or provides valuable information.

- ➢ **Know your brand, know your competition**

Having an effective and efficient brand strategy is what differentiates your business from the competition. Before investing in digital marketing, make sure you build a strong brand. Knowing who you're up against is the best way to stay ahead of the competition—knowing what they offer and how their products are better or worse than yours can help your business stand out. You can use the strengths and weaknesses of your competition to improve your marketing.

- ➢ **Participation and personalization are essential**

Digital marketing is personalized. You have to know your audience and know what works. It is not a matter of being the only one who communicates. Instead, you have to seek user participation. Your goal is to get people to speak on your page, and it is undoubtedly better to have a small community that has involvement compared to a broad audience that does not participate.

- ➢ **Keep your digital home in order**

It has a professional website and sends out regular newsletters. Engage with your community to build social capital through your website, newsletters, and social media channels.

What Not To Do

- ➢ **Don't send spam**

The type of digital marketing that best reaches your audience is the one that opts for consent. You lose when we start to saturate inboxes and fill social media with news every minute. The line between constant effort and spam shouldn't be challenging to draw, although some people still struggle with that. For many, digital marketing should be focused on increasing specific events, such as promotions or offers, and the remainder of the time, reducing at a consistent but less intrusive pace.

> **Don't put "all your eggs in the same basket."**

For digital marketing, results count when it comes to the long term, but this still shouldn't dictate your actions. There are many digital marketing outlets, and some of them will be better for your business than others. Some people prefer to create a monthly newsletter or write articles for partner pages, while others prefer small but regular activity on networks like Twitter, Facebook, or Instagram.

However, if your business naturally takes on a digital marketing type, it may be wise to continue with it even if the results are not what you want. Try different marketing techniques to find out the best way to market your business. Rather than putting "all your eggs in one digital marketing basket," take advantage of the different marketing elements available.

> **Do not "sell."**

People no longer want forced sales. If you're going to nurture healthy interaction and engagement with your target audience, then don't sell your products. Post ideas, concepts, and answers to solutions, first use your content to get their trust. They will then be interested enough to want to know more about what you have to offer.

Conclusion

With the popularization of the Internet, traditional marketing techniques were adapted to the online environment. That is how digital marketing emerged, evolving as rapidly as technology does.

Online marketing uses new media and channels to design strategies that help companies stand out on the Internet and attract more customers. Social media, business blogging, email marketing, Google advertising, and other media are just a few examples of digital marketing.

Therefore, digital marketing is the evolution of traditional marketing. From advertisements on radio, television, or the press, we have moved on to ads on the Internet. From the letters with advertising that flooded our mailboxes, we have moved to email marketing. From live product presentations, we have moved on to webinars and videos on YouTube.

The main difference (and advantage) is that new technologies allow us to design personalized marketing strategies. Analytical tools help us to know our target audience much better. We work with our ideal buyer person or client, offering what they need when they need it throughout the sales funnel. We can even anticipate your future expectations.

In this book, you realized the best digital marketing tips to build your strategy. It is essential to propose campaigns in online channels to have notoriety, generate leads, and conquer the sales you want.

Your client is on the internet. What are you waiting to interact with him?

www.ingramcontent.com/pod-product-compliance
Lightning Source LLC
Chambersburg PA
CBHW060849220526
45466CB00003B/1293